A Bristol Boy, Proud and Blue

Published by Dolman Scott Ltd 2022

Copyright © 2022 Steve Slocombe

All rights reserved. No part of this publication may be reproduced, stored in a retrieval system, or transmitted in any form or by any means, electronic, mechanical, photocopy, recording or otherwise, without prior written permission of the copyright owner. Nor can it be circulated in any form of binding or cover other than that in which it is published and without similar condition including this condition being imposed on a subsequent purchaser.

ISBN: 978-1-915351-10-4

Published by
DolmanScott
www.dolmanscott.com

CONTENTS

EARLY YEARS 1

SCHOOL DAYS 11

THE START OF IT! 36

FOR QUEEN AND COUNTRY 41

THE GOOD AND THE BAD 48

ROVERS EVERYWHERE 57

LEARNING CURVE 60

BACK ON MY BACK 68

BACK IN THE GAME 80

INDEPENDENCE AND HOW TO USE IT 96

HISTORY 104

GROWING UP, BUT NOT AS YOU KNOW IT 106

POWER TO THE PEOPLE 117

MORE OF THE SAME 122

THE BEAUTIFUL GAME 128

BEYOND ELATION 131

WEMBLEY, WEMBLEY 140

ROVERS RETURN 144

DARK DAYS 153

A NEW CHALLENGE 158

MAYBE I NEED TO GROW UP 170

TIME TO TALK 179

NO PLACE FOR THE OLD 184

A DOWNWARD SPIRAL 188

BETTER TIMES TO COME 192

IT'S ALL COMING TOGETHER 199

WHAT DOES IT ALL MEAN? 209

ACKNOWLEDGEMENTS 212

As I have got older, two sayings seem to sum up the grim and turbulent Easton days roaming the streets with my Chelsea road gang and the sometimes more volatile times invading towns around the country and standing defiantly on our sacred Tote End.

'**The older I get, the better I was**' is just a comical saying I once heard, that tells us that, perhaps, things were not always as good as we like to remember. Clouded memories buffed and polished to the right clarity in order to sit well in our conscience. Most of us remember our formative years with 'rose-tinted glasses', when in reality things could have been a more bleak and despairing time than the depths of our memory wishes to reveal. All I knew was the situation I found myself in. I knew we weren't wealthy or privileged, but surely there were many young kids worse off than us. You accept your life for what it is, although I always knew there should be more to life than just eking out a pointless existence.

'**I never thought to run, when perhaps I should have. Now I couldn't run if I wanted to!**' Another daft statement that came to me one day and the start of the inspiration to write this book. With age comes experience, something you can't possess without having experiences. When you are young you have no fear, growing up in an area of deprivation that at the time was recommended to be avoided at all costs if visiting Bristol. Poor lighting and narrow Victorian streets, pitch-black alleyways, a warren of rat runs suitable for all manner of criminal deeds. The inner city areas not fully recovered from the harsh post-war years or indeed the actual war. No more than a mile or two from the bright lights of the city centre. We felt there was a point to prove. We thought we were every bit as good, if not better than the rest. In those dark rundown streets we moved at will, doing anything we cared to in order to create some colour in the murky grey world we lived. We all learn by our mistakes. God knows, I made a few!!!

Nowadays though, Easton, once derided as scruffy and almost a no-go area, has – due to gentrification and spiralling property prices – become somewhat fashionable. It still is rough, blighted by drug and gang crime in parts and decaying, as the fabric of the area hasn't changed much at all, save for the addition of countless splashes of graffiti. Well, with the famed street artist Banksy hailing from our dilapidated area, it's not surprising. Where some say scruffy, the upwardly mobile would say Bohemian or Urban Chic, with an influx of property buyers from the healthcare and teaching professions, initially because Easton's property prices were affordable and the location to the town centre made it very attractive. The arrival of these young professionals eager to make their mark on the neglected neighbourhood also demanded and consequently received an assortment of trendy coffee shops and al fresco dining. St Marks Road was recently voted one of the 'coolest' streets in the country, where twenty to thirty and even forty years ago it was not uncommon to hear running battles as mobs of football fans or disillusioned youth take out their frustrations on anyone or anything.

EARLY YEARS

I was born in a crumbling terraced house just off the Pennywell Road, Easton, in 1960. Bean Street was an inner city cobbled street lined with uniform Victorian houses with no front gardens and built for the working classes. It had managed to avoid the bombs of the Blitz, only to succumb to the new world planners in the 1970s. The new inner ring road cut through my birthplace without a thought, thankfully long after we had left, but mercifully sparing the tall majestic church that sat beside it. Being so young, I can't remember the time living there, just the odd surviving black and white photo of children pushing a huge pram with big overlapping wheels. Maybe I was the passenger on that precarious ride. The first time out in the world, and already in danger. I remember stories of the old Leather Tannery at the end of the road and the accompanying assault on the nostrils it caused, and the pub on the corner called The Beer Cask. Easton was well catered for with back-street boozers back then; the vast majority but not all of which are long gone now.

My parents, childhood sweethearts, had never lived more than two miles from this spot, barring a period of evacuation to Cornwall for my father during the war. I came into the world and became the sibling to a resentful older brother, who, like me, would discover, albeit a year or two earlier, the pure rush of emotions that following the Rovers through thick and thin, mainly thin, would bring. But, as most devoted football fans will testify, loyalty is everything, and once you have your team, it's for life. I have the utmost respect for supporters of lower league and non-league teams that have to survive in the shadow of their more illustrious Premier League neighbours.

I remember Dad taking us to Eastville, home to Bristol Rovers: it must have been 1965 at the latest. He was blue to the core and regaled us with stories of driving to Newcastle in the 50s – 'eleven and a half hours, mind; no motorways then; queued down to Ashley Road for tickets.' One of the stories that was repeated many times, and we lapped it up.

I don't remember the game, the score or the opponents, just the noise and swell of a decent crowd on the Tote End. Good enough for me, hooked and forever consigned to a lifetime of frequent disappointment, occasionally broken by unbridled joy.

At the age of two, my parents decided we should move to the suburbs. Lovely, you say. Not so fast! We were council tenants and the suburb we moved to was Knowle West, an expanse of cheaply built houses filled with the deprived underclass. Friday and Saturday, the locals were drinking and fighting in the cavernous purpose-built pub on the square. The women were as hard, if not harder than the men, and the kids were sent out as street vermin to pester the decent population. We now know that, for us, it was on the wrong side of the river, the physical line dividing Blue and Red, Rovers and City. Mum hated it from day one and got back on the council list to return to the cultural melting pot of inner city living.

Seven long years passed, before our 'dream move' was granted. During that time my brother and I had served an apprenticeship on our street and at Ilminster Avenue Primary School that gave us the tools, even at my tender age of nine, for the return back home across the river.

EARLY YEARS

In my later years, I moved away as a publican and my experiences in that environment were also a tapestry of principally hard work, a good serving of stress and some great fun times. As a licensee, you are basically the fun police: people look to you to provide a safe place for them to enjoy their leisure. Not all customers are that way inclined, though, and it falls on the person behind the bar to maintain order whoever is facing you. I have mentioned this, as those fifteen to twenty years took their toll on the memory and the mind. I know that for some years I followed my own advice to customers who came to me with their various problems (women or money or both) and advocated drinking heavily, preferably in my pub. If nothing else, I was very business-minded.

These are my memories of my life, a time that involved violence, poverty, laughter, the odd criminal deed, and joy, but strangely we never had any real fear, other than the normal trepidation prior to entering a battle with like-minded adversaries. No fear, but why should there be? We participated of our own free will. This is a story of a boy who never felt hard done by through the disadvantaged beginnings and just accepted all that life threw at me. Nothing unusual in my eyes; but, in fact, looking back, it was a miracle I survived at all.

Back then you could get a severe kicking for looking at somebody for more than a millisecond, but usually live to tell the tale. I am the proof.

In the Knowle West Street, where we had moved to, my brother and I were weirdly friends with two other sets of brothers; there was Billy and Phillip Rawling and the Prince brothers, who, by coincidence, had the same Christian names as my brother and I, Dave and Steve. We would go out and about over the fields to Hengrove, the other side of Airport Road. Hengrove and Whitchurch, a little further away, seemed to be much nicer than the estate we had found ourselves living in. Bigger houses and probably the majority were homeowners, as it seemed all the houses were in a better condition than most of the council properties on our side of the busy road. At least at the time that's how I perceived it. At such a young age, it felt like we were on some wild safari trek. There was a great feeling of space, something to be grateful for, and I was going to miss it on our return to the claustrophobic inner city. Occasionally, we would knock on a door of any smart, pristine house to ask for a drink, as every summer seemed to be hot and balmy. No fear or thoughts of being kidnapped and abused by some weirdo. Parents today wouldn't dream of letting their six- or seven-year-olds out to roam the countryside unsupervised.

We rarely had any thought to cause trouble; just climbing trees, fishing in the streams and building dens, probably not unlike countless young boys of a similar age throughout the country. There was even a farm within walking distance, and tormenting the livestock was fun. No real mischief at all, other than the sort of pranks young boys let loose to their own devices and imagination would do. That was the case up until developers started to build a new housing estate on our great wilderness. The lure of the building site one day was too much to resist, and it was there I have one of my earliest recollections of the mischievous nature we had, when Billy, the eldest, called us all to jump onto the dumper truck. He managed to start it up, and without any modicum of skill and no hesitation, crashed it straight through the side wall of the show home.

At that age, I didn't mind running, as we all leapt for our lives and galloped home to the sanctuary of the estate. Other great tricks followed, including wedging four-inch nails under every tyre of the rent man's brand new Morris Minor. Strangely, I don't remember getting into trouble for that one. In fact, there was probably an almighty cheer resonating around the whole of the council estate. Like Robin Hood's tiny gang of merry men. I also have vague recollections of raiding our school at weekends, flitting around like church mice in the eerily quiet school grounds, trying all the doors for access. Why we did, I have no idea, other than the fact that it was there, so why not?

One of my earliest memories was of my parents hosting a Christmas Eve party. My brother and I had been shipped off to bed, but we were unable to sleep because of the impending excitement, of course, but mainly the growing noise emanating from the party downstairs. Inevitably, we crept down to investigate. Unnoticed by the inebriated crowd of Uncles, Aunts and close family friends, we found ourselves under a table partaking in the drinks on offer. For my part, as a six-year-old, I managed to consume a reasonable amount of whisky. God only knows why, as even today I cannot tolerate the taste. Perhaps it was this night that put paid to my relationship with Scotland's finest product. Before anyone noticed or could intervene, I decided to become a gymnast walking the high beam; more accurately the back of the sofa. I had climbed up and briefly started my Olympic display. Within a few steps at most, I went crashing off. Unfortunately for me, I left the apparatus the wrong side, plummeting to the floor behind the sofa. I remember very little after that, and the landing could account for it. As was the way back then, I was picked up, dusted down and returned to bed to sleep off what was to be my very first hangover.

It was around the age of eight I had my first 'fight'. Playing in the Prince brothers' garden, a house brick was lobbed over the hedge from next door. For some unexplained reason, I decided to head it.

A BRISTOL BOY, PROUD AND BLUE

I have had better ideas. One broken brick and 16 stitches in the forehead. I was told it was Roland who did it. I think our gang of siblings promoted the idea of a fight, and with Billy and Dave my brother in my corner coaching me, the match was arranged for a day or two after having the stitches removed.

Roland, by the way was, 13 years old, but probably in age only. I was nothing if not ambitious, fearless and a little bit green.

'Hit him in the guts and knee him in the face,' were the basic instructions from the advisors in my corner.

I left the Blue corner (it would always have to be the Blue corner) and concentrated on putting the master plan into action. To be fair, Roland was a pitiful sight, probably undernourished, and I was astounded he found the strength to heave the brick over the hedge at all. Even at my tender age, the first left swung beautifully into his midriff and he folded double immediately; part two, knees up and smack to the head. Cheers from the baying crowd and bang repeat. I was having a ball watching this human yo-yo going up and down. It felt like ages, but in reality probably wasn't more than a couple of repeated blows, and very quickly he turned away, sobbing and bleeding from his not so prominent nose.

Love a bit of redemption. That's how I perceived it. What was he thinking, chucking a house brick over a hedge?

I think from there on I always like to believe I was the good guy. Hate bullies, later to be joined by another hatred, Bristol City.

EARLY YEARS

It was around this time, before turning nine, I suffered my first major trauma. Running an errand for Mum, I was with some other lad in our street and had to cross the aforementioned Airport Road to get to the shops in Hengrove. This was a fast strip of a concrete slab that acted as a dividing line between the two areas. It ran a good distance all the way from the Wells Road and Whitchurch to Hartcliffe, another sprawling council estate built with high-rise flats for people with low-rise ambitions. If nothing else, I should have been grateful we hadn't moved there, or its equally depressing neighbour Withywood. Both estates expanded to house the workforce for the enormous Wills tobacco factory.

The road, a shiny silver grey ribbon, arced away to my left in a sweeping bend, and I didn't see or hear the motorbike, as the rider crouched low over the tank to get every bit out of his machine that he could. Banking around the bend as he waited to open it up on the urban raceway, he also never saw me, the small child crossing in front of him. I slowed him down quite significantly as, for the first time but not the last, I was catapulted into the air. A lady that witnessed the event guessed I achieved an altitude of 15 foot before plummeting to earth and landing squarely on my head. Miraculously, although I did suffer a fractured skull and the best pair of crusty black eyes ever, I considered myself rather fortunate to have survived.

In hindsight, this incident may well be the catalyst for my future behaviour. A spell in hospital of a week or two. Again, this would not be my last visit to our wonderful National Health Service.

We moved back to Easton in '69. Armstrong was landing on the Moon and we arrived at a different planet to the one we'd left years earlier. The intervening years had not been kind to this already deprived area.

I had no previous reference, having left for the wilds of South Bristol at a very young age, but for me the difference to the wide open spaces we had come from was shocking not only for me, but my brother also.

At least now our grandparents didn't live far away, so, as Mum had also started working again, we had somewhere to go for lunch, usually a tin of soup still in the can, bubbling away in a saucepan of water on the stove, and a chunk of bread for dunking. Grandad Harry was the chef, and the memory of the house is still strong. Their home was another little terrace with a brick-built shed topped with a corrugated roof in the concrete back yard. We sat in the back room – no one ever used the front rooms. Back then it was for visitors that rarely arrived. A huge green sofa and my Grandad sat at a mahogany-coloured dining table with carved pedestal legs. Skipper, the large black crossbreed dog, asleep underneath. On the table, the *Sporting Life*, and the only sounds other than Grandad humming some unrecognisable tune was the sound of the large wall clock slowly ticking. When the radio was put on, it was only in order to listen to the news.

In fact, several of both sides of the family were now within a few miles. Most importantly, though, Eastville Stadium was now within walking distance.

I was enrolled at Bannerman Road School, a tall, grey, flaking Victorian building that had long passed its prime. The interior of the building had fared slightly better, other than the chunks and digs taken out of the walls and woodwork courtesy of years and years of children's attention. The wide shiny corridors and the assembly hall, however, had retained the parquet flooring and was polished to a bright but weathered shine. All of the tall windows were way above the reach and view of primary school children. Outside, all the play areas were grey tarmac, not a blade of grass to be seen.

I longed for the wide open spaces of Hengrove and Airport Road, or even the long gardens bordered with thick privet hedges we had in Knowle West.

From the playground, you could see and hear the trains on the rails above us, thundering by or just picking up momentum after slewing their way out of Temple Meads station, a couple of miles away down the line. With over six tracks and Stapleton Road railway station less than four hundred yards away, the rumble and click-clack from the main line was constant. From the disadvantaged view we had in the playground, even the embankment, the only hue of green, was hidden by the crusty school walls that were topped with a wire fence that had been twisted and ravaged by years of unruly playground activity.

On the first day, the poverty was obvious: undernourished scrawny kids in scuffed shoes and tatty trousers. I went in goal in the playground, in a jumpers-for-goalposts game. Unfortunately, while making a cat-like save, I stepped on a goalpost and the owner decided to have a pop at the Knowle West boy. Robert Michaels stepped forward, windmill-flailing, and a frantic little exchange went off. Welcome to Easton. Obviously, no one got really hurt – we were only nine – but I stepped up, as I always would, never a thought to back down. I'd made a mark. Rob and I later became great friends throughout our school days.

We lived in Battersea Road at the end of Chelsea Road, the same as all the other roads there: terrace after terrace, and even a sprinkling of old miners' cottages, narrow houses with tiny doors and windows, a reminder of the colliery long abandoned and closed in 1911. Several of the terrace houses were painted in odd garish colours, reflecting the multitude of different nationalities. Even at the end of the sixties and start of the seventies, Easton was a hugely cosmopolitan community.

At the top of Chelsea Road stood a large red-brick building. Casting a shadow down from high, The Owen Street Mission, a once-proud building flanked by the homes of its congregation, now standing almost alone as the small 2-up 2-down houses made way for development that never came. The Mission stood defiantly in the increasing sea of rubble and waste, slowly losing its veneer and fading away. It was where we'd hope to find salvation in the Boys' Brigade, but we only found the tuck shop to pilfer from after hiding under the stage and waiting for the place to be locked up. Sneaking out to raid the cupboards, we had no thought to how we'd escape. There were no sophisticated alarm systems back then, though, so any window or door would do. It didn't take long for the thefts to get noticed, and we were dismissed from the Brigade; the bugle had to go back. Next stop: the Saint Gabriel Cubs. I wondered what their tuck shop would be like.

SCHOOL DAYS

The schools I attended were quite unremarkable, other than the fact they were all filled with solid deprived working-class kids. After Ilminster Avenue and Bannerman Road came the big school. St George Comprehensive was the destination for the inner city area we lived in. It was here that new friends and enemies were forged.

St George at the time was on several sites. I started at Avonvale Road for the first year, managing to have a punch-up on the first day, but with who I can't remember. Nothing serious, but I got the impression that kids from Easton were looked down on. I wasn't having that, and the row in the playground set me fair for my senior school days. It was here, though, that I started to get to know lads from St Anne's and Barton Hill, along with others from St George and Redfield. My cheeky side started to make an appearance, too, when asking our French teacher, Mr Eagle, to fly down off his perch and answer my question. A pal and I were banished from the classroom for the first time; we spent the rest of the period climbing the trees outside, trying not to be noticed by the headmaster out and about on his patrols.

For the following two years we were transferred to the Park School. This tall, imposing red-brick building stood, as the name suggests, on the edge of St George Park. The headmaster, Mr Long, ruled with an iron fist, and I'm sure he fancied himself as some sort of powerful Soviet dictator. A short man with broad shoulders and a steely blue-eyed stare, he instilled fear into his poor 11- to 14-year-old subjects.

The park itself was our cross country course; at the far end from the top by the library, it descended down a large grassy valley and then up the other side. Even in the height of summer, it was a quagmire. Mr Long's evil sidekick, a Welsh Physical Education instructor called Mr Brierley, used the mud-splattered bodies as an indication that we were following the correct route. Three times around the park to satisfy his mean streak. A few of us always ran in the middle of the pack, and on the second lap would peel off and sit down a little lane until they all came around again, always ensuring we finished nowhere near the front or the back.

There were several teachers of note, some good and some with a sadistic streak. The latter favoured different methods of inflicting pain. One of them, a History teacher, used to enjoy pulling his victims off the floor by the sideburns. Another would regularly throw the blackboard eraser at anyone without any fear or compunction of injuries he might cause. The same teacher once blew a fuse and stomped up to a disruptive pupil and tore his workbooks in half, before launching them out of the open window overlooking the main road. But the Lex Luther of my school days was the commandant, Mr Long.

One Friday after assembly, he stood singling out boys with long hair. This was probably 1974, and in total around 30 sacrificial lambs were selected. I was one of them. All three term years were represented, with my third year having the most offenders.

We were all ordered to have a haircut over the weekend and he would be around the classrooms on Monday morning to inspect each and every one of us.

I went home at the end of the day and told Dad what was expected. 'You tell him, if he wants you to have your hair cut, he can pay for it,' said Dad. All right for you to say that, I thought, but if that's what he wants me to say, I will.

Dreading Monday morning and thoroughly disappointed to see most had had the good old short back and sides, I went to my first lesson of the day. I was in the science lab right at the top of the building and starting to relax, when the door at the front of the classroom creaked open.

I was already rising from my seat and moving towards the crisp shiny suit of Herr Long.

Outside in the hallway, with my back firmly against the wall, I waited for him to saunter out of the classroom, before he enquired as to why I hadn't obeyed his instructions. '**Well, my… my Dad said, if you wants me to get my hair cut… you can pay for it!!**' I mumbled limply.

'You what?' he yelled, and the sound echoed around the building. Everything fell silent as he then bawled, 'Get outside my office now.'

Off I ran at a gallop down the wide stairwell's three floors, barely touching the majority of steps, until I reached the shiny mahogany door to my left. I turned and stood against the beige wall with the door now to my right and the foot-worn grey stone staircase in front of me. I waited an age as he patrolled the corridors, seeking more disobedient youths. Unfortunately for me, I was the only rebel he found that day, and eventually he reappeared. Slithering down the stairs with his stare fixed on me, he glided past like a ghost and opened the door to his office, disappearing without a word.

The door was ajar, and peeking in, I caught a glimpse of the opulent lair. 'In!' he shouted and I entered. To my right and left were comfortable-looking wingback chairs and all around the room were tall book cabinets matching the dark mahogany of the door. The light shone in from a wide window to my left and the floor felt soft as I walked on the thick-pile carpet. In front of me, sat behind a cavernous desk, and behind him a mass of diplomas, was Mr Long. Again he said nothing for an age as he pulled out a packet of No.6 cigarettes and slowly removed one. He placed it in his mouth and struck a match. Letting the flame settle, he lit the cigarette and took a deep tug. The end of the fag glowed as if accusing me of some heinous crime. He eventually exhaled and a cloud of smoke partially masked us for a second or two. This Gestapo-like interrogation was worse than the final punishment, which was always some corporal punishment of a few swipes across the hand with his favourite cane or trainer. 'Now, what did you say again?' he drawled in a softer but more menacing tone. I feebly managed to repeat what I had said at the top of the stairs, but not with as much conviction. After the hand-stinging, we agreed that maybe I should get my hair cut. I didn't, though.

Almost ten years later, I was playing a pool or darts match in the Bell pub in Stapleton and I was walking back from the bar with a couple of pints of cider. The teachers were on strike at the time and a group were having a meeting in the pub. A short, stocky man walking towards me playfully punched me in the stomach and said, 'Still soft' as he did so. It was Mr Long.

I immediately said, 'Did you notice I never spilt a drop? Who's the soft one, Longy?' Incredible that he recognised me after all that time.

SCHOOL DAYS

After the Park School, we moved on to the Upper School. This was on Russell Town Avenue and was much closer to home than the others. There was no such thing as a school-run back then. If it was a long way, you had to leave home earlier.

The school classes were banded as the number of students were quite high. It basically meant that there were two classes banded together as a similar level. The class letters were loosely based on the motto of 'Can Be Just'. The top band, or highest classes, became C,A,N,X, followed by B,E,J, etc.

I found myself in 'X'. The first year at the Upper School, or fourth year, was quite uneventful. Again, finding yourself in another building, albeit the same school, takes time to adjust. Pupils had arrived not only from The Park, but also another site in Rose Green.

My arrival at the Upper School was noted during our first technical drawing lesson with the wiry Mr Ramsey. Whilst reading the register, he announced my name and I duly replied.

'Stephen Slocombe!' he enquired… 'Any relation to David Slocombe?'

'Yes, sir, he's my brother.' Dave had just left to start his apprenticeship, but in truth he had left months and months earlier, preferring the delights of the local Coral's or Ladbrokes to education.

'Well,' he shouted, 'let me tell you what your brother has done with his chances of success in this life.'

He leapt onto his desk and proceeded to tear a bundle of paper into shreds, throwing the resulting confetti high into the air.

Very impressive display, I thought, but it was incumbent on me to inform Mr Ramsey of my brother's apprenticeship, and also that he was probably already earning more than a comprehensive school teacher. The class erupted, and we were all then shouted down by the insulted professional, and I instantly became enemy number one. Well, he started it!!

The final year was a different time entirely. City had achieved some success by getting promoted to the First Division, and suddenly everyone was a shithead (City fan). As pure luck would have it, our class and class 'N' were predominately Rovers supporters, and a bit of class rivalry started. This quickly escalated to full-scale battles practically anywhere around the school. In the changing room, outside classes and on the stairwells were all happy hunting grounds. The teaching staff had no control as the battles would sometimes spill into the classrooms. Walking around school on your own became very unwise, as you would get jumped by members of C or A. I can still hear the smashing of the lockers as we were throwing each other against them. One day, a mass brawl was arranged behind the sports hall at lunch time and we all assembled like *Zulu Dawn*. I led the charge, and a huge bundle ensued. Every time one of these scraps happened, I always found myself selecting some City fan to have a pop at. I'm sure it was the same for those lads, too. No weapons were ever used; it was just a good old-fashioned punch-up. However, one lunchtime, a large group of us met on the stairs and off it went as usual. Unfortunately, this time one lad was thrown over the rail and plummeted a floor or two, breaking his leg in the process.

After this, a full assembly was organised and all the combatants were threatened with expulsion. Things calmed down a bit after that, not because of the threat of losing the place at school, but more that although we were kicking seven shades out of each other, to us it was just fun and we never really wanted anyone to get properly hurt.

Most years, Mum and Dad always managed to book a holiday for us to Cornwall, and sometimes we would be accompanied by my Nan and an Uncle, Aunt and their husbands. Dad never had a car reliable enough to make the long journey (there were no motorways, mind), so he would always hire a car, and the excitement of what sort of luxury vehicle he would pick up was the start of our great holiday.

Invariably, the luxury was non-existent, practicality being the watchword for the charabanc needed to transport at least eight to that wonderful county. Fords seemed the most common choice, with the Consul or Zodiac models favoured because of the bench seat at the front and cavernous boot space.

We would leave at a ridiculous time of the morning, sometimes not much after midnight. Dad had probably worked the day before and would be impatiently itching to get down there. At forty or so miles an hour, with a stop for breakfast in a transport café, we would eventually arrive at either a caravan park or some glorious detached property with a garden the likes of we could never imagine.

One year, staying at Hayle Towans Caravan Park, we, as usual, arrived while it was still dark, with the sun just beginning to show a red hue in the distance, promising a glorious day ahead. We started our crawl along the rows of beautiful, shiny new mobile homes, each with their large square picture windows with the curtains still drawn.

'What number are we?' asked Dad.

Mum replied, '368. That one is 360; lovely, isn't it, Ivor?'

Dave and I started to count the caravans, as the rest of the car's passengers commented on how nice that one was, and 'Look, that un's lovely, in all.'

362, lovely; 363, gorgeous; 364, phew what a beauty!!! Then we arrived at 368, the runt of the litter. Big enough sure, but no big picture window or large square profile. This grey sloping mongrel of a caravan even had a thin chimney poking out of the top.

All too tired to worry, we piled in to investigate. The layout was such that my Auntie and Nan had a separate bedroom at the end, Uncle and his wife another dividable space. My brother and I slept in the dining area after converting the plywood table; and Mum and Dad were in the kitchen area. It had a convertible sofa that when pulled out left no more than a foot-wide gap between them and the stove.

Dad thought it was marvellous, because he would lean over around six in the morning and put the kettle on. It would be whistling around 7.30! One unfortunate morning, though, as Dad rolled back, the bed separated down the middle and then snapped back shut, trapping a very sensitive part of his anatomy. The yelp of pain woke the whole caravan, and probably the next three or so either side of us. That was one of two unfortunate incidents to befall him on that holiday. The second was on a gloriously hot day on the huge expanse of sand at Hayle. I had already fallen victim to the sun's power. I'm sure Mum tried to protect us, but Ambre Solaire, if it existed, would have been so expensive, so when my shoulders and back became covered in blisters, I was wrapped in Dad's shirt and told to have a lie down. It was while I was curled up, hoping for an ice cream to take the pain away, that Dad, also asleep and out for the count, was targeted by a precision-bombing seagull that managed a direct hit into his mouth. Jumping up and spluttering, the expletives were of the kind I had never heard from him before. The laughing from all of us bar one, Dad, strangely helped to ease my pain, and we all got ice creams, mainly to take the taste away for Dad.

Then, on another holiday to Marazion, near St Michael's Mount, we had rented a large bungalow with a huge mature garden. It was football most days on the lawn, and when we tired of that, Dave and I decided to investigate the wonders of the greenhouse. I've never liked tomatoes, but we stole them all anyway. Some of the other vegetables on display I had never seen before, so the courgettes and peppers were left untouched. Even to this day I don't see the point of courgettes – tasteless and watery, the devil's veg in my opinion. Predictably, a stray kick took out a glass pane, but we kept quiet about it, hoping it wouldn't be noticed.

During the stay, Dad and his youngest brother, our Uncle Mervyn, had gone out for a while, and Mervyn's future wife decided to play a trick. I was only around twelve, and they dressed me up in high heels, jewellery and a long sweater with a golden chain-style belt, topped off with wig and all the make-up required. I posed for photos, then removed the entire seventies ensemble before they returned. My future Auntie Angela did a convincing role as the betrayed fiancée, sobbing, 'Who is that woman who came here looking for you?'

Mervyn, bewildered and not believing a word, protested his innocence.

'Wait 'til you see the photo, then!' Which would have to wait until Boots had done their job when we returned from holiday.

My Mum and Auntie kept the pretence up for about two days, before releasing him from his torment. The photo, when it was developed, was quite convincing; and thinking about it now, a little disconcerting for me, as I looked quite good.

Group holidays seemed to be the norm for the time. Family from my Mum's side – and there were plenty of them, as both my parents came from large families and had produced a multitude of offspring (I have enough cousins to fill a concert hall) – would book sometimes twenty people into Butlin's at Barry Island. They would all arrive on a Saturday and occupy a block of chalets, and we would go over with Mum and Dad on Sunday morning for a visitor day. At five in the evening, Mum and Dad would depart and leave us with the family for a free week's holiday.

All was well until we had a disagreement with some other kids on the camp and Dave, my cousin Kevin and I were rounded up by security.

We were hauled away from the arcade and the Pig and Whistle pub, straight into the security office. The pokey little room was filled with sweaty, overweight, not-good-enough-to-be-a-copper types who relished the perceived power they now possessed. The sun shone brightly through a plain window, silhouetting a large, rotund man who, rather worryingly during his initial questioning, was polishing the end of his arm, as his hand was missing. All I could think at the time was, **'I hope he doesn't hit me with his wrist.'** It sent a shiver down my spine.

After a long lecture and some deriding comments about the youth of Bristol, we were released back to the bosom of our family. We managed to stay for the week without getting caught for anything else!! So much for the finger-on-the-pulse security – they didn't even figure out that we shouldn't have been on the site at all.

***

After a period of settling into life back in Easton, Dave found his group of mates around the local streets and I found mine. Our gang was the next generation, so to speak, and was initially just a few of us from no more than four or five streets. We expanded our 'gang' after a row over the bonfire we were building on waste ground by the railway arch. This was the preferred spot for several other lads that lived towards the bottom end of Chelsea Road, and we had commandeered their site for our use. This, of course, was back in the day when you were allowed to build huge monolithic structures to burn and fire rockets down the street at each other. Bangers thrown into the phone boxes and holding the door shut was always entertaining. To protect our work, we would quite often spend the night in them, because they were often targets for other kids to burn down prior to the big day. The effort we put into securing the materials to burn, whether the donors wanted us to have the stuff or not, along with the actual assembly, was immense, and we wanted it protected.

Of course, kids today aren't allowed to do anything remotely risky. They are all protected by the nanny state we live in or over-protective parents. Christ, even Conkers have been outlawed. Try it today and you'd be carted off for assessment on your social delinquency or some other convoluted mental tag placed on the young by the sanctimonious authorities. The bonfire site dispute was simply sorted out with a couple of punches, and we became a bigger gang that would remain tightly knitted into our early twenties.

The members were great mates: Ken (Tater), Terry, Mark, Steve, Sean, Wayne, Rich, and myself were the core of the group. To this day, although we have all gone our separate ways, Steve in particular is still a very close friend.

Terry and Mark Iron were brothers, and their parents were the most understanding and tolerant people I'd ever met. We would regularly have parties at their house, and as Mark was acknowledged as the best looking, we always had plenty of girls in attendance. **'The older I get, the better I was.'** I would like to think some of the female attendees were mainly interested in me, but in reality Mark was their main target, and the rest of us would do our best to entertain the surplus. Their parents would go out and come back late enough for us to have ejected most of the 'guests', and just in time to help with putting the last of the doors back on. Mrs Iron would then say, 'Who'd like something to eat?' She would produce huge bowls of chilli and chunks of crusty bread. Wonderful people – maybe just their Italian heritage.

The first death and funeral I think any of us experienced was when Terry and Mark's amazing grandfather passed away. He was always there talking with the boys: great stories from the old country. He had insisted he wanted us all at his funeral, and, of course, we were honoured to pay our respects. As I arrived at the house, just a small end of terrace tucked away at the very top of their road, with a tiny front garden no more than three foot deep from pavement to front door, as were most houses in the narrow, dark back streets of Easton, I was taken aback by the numbers of people crushed into the back room and kitchen, as well as swarming around in the street outside. Family and friends from all parts had arrived; London and Italy were represented. The house was packed, except the front room, where our friends' dear grandfather was resting. We were all asked if we would like to see him, and some declined. Death has never concerned me, even though I never knew so at the time, and I was grateful for the chance to say goodbye.

I counted eight main funeral hearses and a further twenty-seven cars following the procession to the ceremony at St Mary on the Quay, on the Centre, and then on to Canford Crematorium for the interment. We were being driven in a sporty little Escort by one or other older cousin. More Italian-looking than Terry or Mark, he was wearing some, at the time, fashionable tight leather driving gloves with an open back and stud-button fastener. As the cortege left the Church of St Mary on the Quay on the Centre and swung around to leave via Park Street, en route to the Crematorium, we were the first car behind the funeral hearses, and as we started to climb the little incline onto Park Street, an unconnected motorist attempted to cut in front of us. Our tanned driver immediately swung his steering wheel left and then sharp to the right, ramming the side of the invading motorist. The other car swung away and retreated away behind us. Later, after the interment, our Italian chauffeur 'Giusseppe' drove to a local Police Station to report that he had his car rammed while driving in a funeral procession. Outrageous!!! He said, 'What awful behaviour, showing no respect...', etc, etc.

During our early teenage school days, at weekends our gang used to go walkabout in a similar fashion to the trips in Knowle West. But this time we had to go further to find any green space, and Eastville Park through to Snuff Mills was a favourite haunt. I'm sure we never went to look for trouble, but we could find it lurking anywhere. One day, during our exercise regime, we were near the bottom of Eastville Park, under the shadow of the invasive grey concrete of the M32 motorway overpass. Around two hundred yards away, we waved at a figure we thought we recognised; but as the mystery man approached, we realised we didn't after all, and said so. This unknown Lone Ranger took umbrage and started to engage in an argument with this motley group of kids. It didn't take long before I was singled out and challenged. I was happy to oblige him and, of course, stepped up with eagerness and immediately engaged in a brawl with him. '**I never thought to run, when perhaps I should have.**' My mantra reared its head not for the first time, as this bloke was easily late teens or early twenties, larger and stronger than me. I quickly realised I might get a bit of a hiding and prepared myself for that. Then, though, the lads that were with me decided to assist; not the most honourable thing to do, but it saved me in that instance from being choked to death. A swift salvo of kicks and punches saw him off.

We continued on our route march, laughing aloud and satisfied we had seen a little bit of 'action'; but little did we know there was more to come. Walking away from the lake towards Snuff Mills, we took the long, winding path, with the stream on one side down a steep embankment and a bank rising up and away on the other side. Before you get right to Snuff Mills, there is a little bridge to take you over the stream, and away to the right a little cave. Tall, majestic trees encircle this glade... all very picturesque. Probably the reason we liked going there, to get away from the narrow, dilapidated, rundown Easton streets, where the only open spaces were mainly courtesy of the Luftwaffe.

We heard a shout and looked in the direction it came from. At the top of the hill we could identify the Lone Ranger; he was accompanied by Tonto and several other deputies. They all looked to be of a similar stature to the masked sheriff, but more concerning was the large machete-sized objects being brandished in the air and catching a reflection from the sun. In this instance, on our toes seemed the better option, and through the river the best escape. It's safe to say we gave the park a wide berth for a couple of weeks.

Around this time, age 14, I had started going to Rovers with other friends from school, and my first away trip was looming. Plymouth on the train – I couldn't wait. What a wonderful thing the football special was. The arrival in a strange town was well rehearsed and orchestrated to a tee. Maximum noise and carnage, hope to out-run the law, roll a car or two on the rowdier days, and introduce yourselves to the local competition.

But before the joys of inter-city travel, my education in the heart of Bristol continued.

Our parents were hard-working, honest people who had a grasp on the real world. Dad was raised in Easton and evacuated in the war, and my Mother grew up in neighbouring St Werburghs, but stayed at home throughout the worst the Germans could throw at us. They allowed us the freedom to do what we pleased, with just one caveat: 'Don't bring any trouble home.' Well, I did my best, but it was a difficult task.

One summer holiday, the gang decided we would get the train to Severn Beach for a spot of swimming in the Lido. Even then, as the train pulled in to the end of the line, I thought, 'Is this the end of the world?' A little swim in the open air in the shadows of oil refineries at Avonmouth is not the sort of place to send a 'wish you were here' postcard from. The pool was littered with broken bottles, and the rusty chain-mail fence surrounding it, along with the flaking beige paint, looked like it had given up all hope. It will never be Weston-

Super-Mare, that's for sure!!! It looked desperate, but we were there to have a good time. Several hours of splashing around and trying to chat up the local girls, without much success, we then made our way the couple of hundred yards to the train station. Even here, waiting for the train to go home, we managed to pick a row with the locals. They gave us a bit of a lesson in respect and we showed them a cocky attitude and no respect at all. We boarded the train vowing to return. We did. A fortnight later, we had rallied the troops and most of the school boarded the Shithole Express to Severn Beach. We were going to show those fuckers!!!

A lovely sunny day, and the best part of 50 scraggly teenagers with attitude disembarked at the world's worst seaside resort. The 'hook a duck' stall put the boards up, which was probably half the available entertainment gone for the day. We made our way to the swimming pool and were nervously allowed in to sun our pasty sun-starved bodies.

No locals to be seen. Where were they? Some of the St Ann's and Barton Hill boys asked, a strange truce between the two warring areas.

It was shortly after that we started to hear a low rumble getting louder and louder. It built to a crescendo – the unmistakable sound of Harley-Davidsons. The splashing about ceased, and we looked at the rusty chain-link fence. One after another, big, hairy, leather-clad bodies appeared all along the fence. 'Looks like the locals have better back-up than we do,' I thought to myself. We heard a growling voice advising us to fuck off back to Bristol. We were very happy to oblige. The Police arrived to escort us, which, without admitting it, we were quite grateful for. I don't even remember anyone giving it large from the train window as we sloped away. So much for sorting them out. We were so far out of our depth, and I don't mean in the swimming pool.

As we got a little older, around 15, I had a taste of the excitement of going to the football with my mates, and I started to find my desire to stand and fight. One summer's evening, our little gang was patrolling our area, which stretched into Whitehall, Devon Road and beyond to Packers playing fields, all connected by a disused railway line; which, as it ran right along the top of our street, was a useful escape route more than once when being pursued by the local constabulary.

For some unknown reason, one of the lads with us decided to snap an aerial off a car. I was unaware until we reached a junction just around the corner from Terry and Mark's. We heard a bit of shouting and looked around to see three huge men running full pelt at us around 150 to 200 yards away. On closer inspection, they were all carrying rather large pieces of 4 x 2 wood and waving them like demented demons. I stood my ground without a thought to run and looked behind me to check on the boys. I just caught a glimpse of a green flash trainer disappearing around the corner! What to do now? I may have nerve, but I like to think I am reasonably intelligent. Self-preservation became the order of the day, so I looked around for options. On the corner there was a shop with a crate of empty milk bottles. I grabbed a couple and defiantly threw them generally in the direction of my assailants. Then, on my toes after my brave troops. I vividly remember laughing out loud as I passed Mark and Terry frantically scrambling for their front-door key as I sprinted on past Bloy Street, Colston Street and Chelsea Park to my escape route: the railway. I caught a glimpse of Rich and Tater diving to the right down the narrow alley between the two roads. I took a quick look as they scrambled over the various amounts of dumped rubbish in the darkness and then vanished from sight into the night.

As we started to get older, my brother and I drifted apart. In truth, we were never very close when we were young; as I said, he was resentful when I was born and this continued throughout our school days. Fights between us were common, and when we were younger I usually came off worse. People who know me may not believe this, but I was a quiet child, happy with my own company. As children, Dave would torment me mercilessly. Eventually, the worm was going to turn, and the biggest punch-up between us came when he had left school and he was around 17. I was a fit and healthy 15-year-old and had gained some confidence along with stature, as I was now taller and broader than him. Not that either of us were giants.

One Sunday afternoon, Dave came home from the pub and retrieved his lunch from the oven. He placed it on a small table in the lounge and just got up and turned the TV over without asking Mum if she minded. I did, and got up and turned it back to the programme Mum had been watching, saying so in the process. To be honest, back then there were probably only two or three channels to pick from. He once again got up and turned it back over, and I repeated the action. At this point, he started to wipe his knife and then wave it in my direction. We both leapt to our feet and started swinging. In the melee, with Mum shouting and trying to separate us, she unfortunately got an elbow in the jaw and stumbled back, but I didn't give ground and continued flailing away. Eventually, Dave broke off and headed for the bathroom. I pursued him, kicking a hole in the bathroom door in an attempt to get at him and continue. After a short while, I began to calm down and I went back downstairs to see how Mum was. Not surprisingly, she was very upset that, once again, we had gone at it, and this time left a large arc of blood across the lounge wall and a Sunday roast sprawled across the carpet. These events, although they made me so annoyed, also upset me, and I would usually retreat to my bedroom to sulk. Dave had disappeared out in order to avoid our father when he got home, and it was after this latest row that I really felt Dad's anger.

He returned from the traditional Sunday lunch pub visit a little later and, seeing the carnage we had left, climbed the stairs and, with a few choice words, punched me full in the side of the head. I heard bells, whistles and notably saw stars as my head rebounded off the wall. I still remember that punch even to this day, but totally understand why he did it and agreed it was probably justified. This dislike between my brother and I continued until I was 17 and suffered another big trauma, another motorbike accident, but this time I was riding it. This seemed to make us closer, and I'm pleased to say it continues to this day.

***

Dave left school at 16. In truth, he was very rarely there, preferring the education on offer at the local betting shops. He did, as mentioned earlier, secure an apprenticeship as a tiler, a job of work he would do throughout his life. He'd bought his first car: a shaky, damp-ridden Triumph Herald. He loved it, but I hated it because of the number of times I had to push it the length of not only our street but most of the way down Chelsea Road to bump-start it.

'Come on, give us a push. I'll drop you off at school when it starts.' It rarely started, and I'd still have to walk to school. But we are eternal optimists, and push it we did.

He eventually replaced most of the engine and the reliability improved a little; so much so that he decided to take it to Torquay. Rovers were playing on the Saturday evening at Plainmoor, home to Torquay United. The weather was glorious and we planned to stay down overnight. No thought for accommodation, just a chance to catch an away game. Five of us piled into the tiny car and off we rumbled. As soon as got there, we headed for town to find a pub, aptly named The Bristolian. Should be a friendly welcome in there, we thought. All was well, and as young kids, 'Tater', Rich and myself sat at the back as my older brother got the drinks in. He had brought one of his mates with him – a tough, broad, black guy called Charlie. A few years later we would all frequent the Dog House Disco at Eastville most weeks. Well, at least the weeks we weren't barred for causing some sort of trouble. The door staff were a little wary of Charlie, and we took full advantage. The way it would pan out would be:

'You're all barred. Don't you dare come within a mile of this place.'

The following week, we would rock up around 10ish on a quieter Thursday, after a few in the Dirty Duck (Black Swan). And the same bouncers would swing open the doors for us, saying, 'No trouble tonight, lads' – more in hope than anything.

The Bristolian pub was filling up with Gasheads (Rovers fans) and the singing started. The bar was a sort of semi-basement: quite dark, considering the bright sunshine outside. A rumour started circulating that the landlord, who had gone to the trouble of pinning up Rovers scarfs and banners, would do exactly the same if City were playing; and, in fact, he was actually a Shithead (City fan) himself. Probably bollocks, but the next we knew, a fruit machine had been pulled to the floor and several glasses chucked at the bar. The friendly welcome was withdrawn and the pub closed, leaving nothing else but to head for the beach.

The beach itself was rammed with Rovers fans. The largest football match in history was starting with around one hundred-plus a side. Towels for goalposts were requisitioned from bewildered sunbathing tourists and a game with very little skill and even less finesse got under way. After the actual professional match, where a group of Rovers fans had made their way onto the, and I say this flippantly, Torquay End, the aptly named Cowshed, and scattered the home fans far and wide, we had to decide where we were going to get our heads down for the night.

As we cruised the streets of Torquay, taking in the harbour and beach areas, we could see the multitude of Gas (Rovers fans) staggering around, all looking for reasonable shelter for the night. The police were everywhere and appeared to be moving people on, not allowing anyone to settle. So we drove on out of central Torquay and along the coast a little way. My brother pulled the car into some sort of caravan Holiday Park. He stopped in a central open area, switched off the ignition and was asleep in seconds. I couldn't stand the confined space, stuck in the middle on the back seat, and just had to get out. Rich and Tater also got out. Charlie managed to stretch out his large frame and was also snoring as we moved away from the car. I'd noticed a dark arch that seemed to lead towards the coast, so I said I was going to have a look for somewhere to sleep. The other two decided to hunt around the row after row of dimly lit caravans to 'see what we can find'.

As I walked up through the tunnel, I could hear the waves crashing below me. I found myself on a grassy cliff-top in the pitch black. Not thinking it wise to walk any further, I decided this was going to be my bed, and found the flattest bit of ground I could. The sound of the sea was quite relaxing and I fell into a fitful sleep. Several times during the four or so hours that I lay there, I would stir after hearing a strange noise, and through bleary eyes spot all sorts of wildlife, including the silhouettes of the odd rat, bird-life and a fox, scuttling around me. With the morning barely breaking through, I staggered back to the car not even remotely refreshed. We all gathered together in a silent group while, for the smokers, the first intake of nicotine was taken. The car was started and as we passed the Camp Shop we spotted breakfast had been delivered in the shape of a case of milk and a couple of baskets of bread and croissants. We quickly liberated our most important meal of the day and made our getaway.

As poor Easton boys, it was all we could do as 14- to 15-year-olds to get together enough cash for a flagon of NATCH to knock back sitting on top of some garages and reflect on how great life was. We knew no better, after all. To the uninformed, Natch then was called Natural Dry Cider, made in Taunton and also referred to as Riot Soup in some pubs. In order to support our increasing apple dependency, we would locate vacant houses and liberate valuable items. Copper or lead pipe and roof tiles were easily sold at the local scrapyard, and the railway yards at Lawrence Hill were also good hunting grounds. More than once, though, we wished the water had been turned off before we started wrestling with the copper and lead pipes. The site of a discarded rug floating in a couple of inches of water in the lounge was comical to see. We were also very grateful if the outgoing tenants were good enough to leave a couple of old curtains for us to put the 'swag' in.

During one of these house raids, no more than 100 yards from Terry and Mark's house, we had decided to remove a few roof tiles. With no concern for the integrity of the house, we started pulling away the roof felt and battens to get at our 25p prizes. We had taken around twenty, passing them down through the hatch onto the landing. Tater was on tile-removal duty and had made a big enough hole to stand up in order to reach our 'cider tokens'. As he climbed through to grab another, he was in full view of the street below, but luckily not spotted by the coppers in the patrol car passing by at that very second. Even so, we abandoned the scavenger hunt for the day, returning to collect our booty from the garden the next day.

Around 1974/75, a youth club opened up on Russell Town Avenue. In the beginning, the Venturers' Youth Club had hundreds of members, and some of the older guys there carried big reputations. Rob Michael's cousin was one of them. Much older than us, he would arrive in a different car most nights with an entourage of shady characters. His group were easily all in their 20s and commanded a lot of respect. More than once he would take a belt to some of the boys slightly older than us that we considered tough. I won't go into the type of business these guys were involved in, but leave it for the reader to decide. When the club was full, the atmosphere was great. When the music was blasting out, it had more of a feel of a night club. The sounds of the seventies mixed with great SKA and reggae music. Steve Harley and Cockney Rebel's 'Judy Teen' was particularly memorable for the heavy echoing beat. On a quieter night there, though, just our gang of lads and a few others were there. I came back from the toilets to hear Rich and his brother Sean having an almighty row. Although Sean was physically bigger, his brother Rich was quite an unstable character, having once aimed a shotgun at his father's crotch with the intention of never having any more baby brothers or sisters. He was brandishing a knife and people were standing off. As I said before, I hate bullies, so I got involved – much, I imagine, to Sean's relief. I managed to land a good punch as it escalated and Rich hit the floor face-down. Without thinking, I dived onto him, I guess to restrain him. He then managed to swing the knife back and stabbed me in the back of my left leg. Typically, my only thought was that he'd ruined a brand-new pair of jeans. I got up, he swung again and I kicked him squarely in the chest. At that moment, the youth worker grabbed him and threw him through the door and locked us in. Rich then laid a one-man siege to the club, throwing whatever he could at the building. By the time the police arrived, he had calmed down and was back in the club, apologising to me and the youth workers and anyone else that was interested. With blood stains down the back of the left leg of my jeans, I made a point of sitting down as the Police asked who had the knife. We explained there wasn't one and it was just an argument between the two brothers that had got out of hand. They seemed to swallow our story and left. Later, Rich came with me to the hospital whilst I got some stitches in the wound.

I also had a less serious and quite comical row with Tater one afternoon. As kids, you fall out now and again, and I have no idea what caused this one; but off it went, with the both of us exchanging blows and having a little wrestling match in the street. Tater broke off and ran to a high wall a few yards from us. He had spotted a brick at the top and reached for it, with the intention, I imagine, of braining me with it. (Didn't work for Roland a few years earlier.) It was when he tried to pull it away we realised it was cemented on and the opportunity for me to swing a high kick to the back of his head was too good to turn down. My foot connected with his head and subsequently his face with the wall.

SCHOOL DAYS

This was just an example of how things were: never letting any disagreement last too long. With the row with Rich, It didn't hurt, the jeans were ruined, but we got over it and hardly mentioned it again.

As 1975 wore on, we all started thinking about what to do after school. College and University weren't even in our vocabulary. Where we lived, you went to school, you left and went to work or prison. For myself, I had always had a wish to join the Army. I don't know where it came from, but it was always there. I started talking about it, and my brother Dave challenged me to do something about it. I thought I would, so, although I was doing well at school and, unlike my brother, I actually enjoyed it and attended all the time, I took myself off to the recruitment building on the centre. The following January I was given train travel to Corsham in Wiltshire for three days of assessments. At the end I had earned an apprenticeship with the Royal Engineers at Beachley Camp under the Severn Bridge, starting in September, no more than two weeks after my 16th birthday. I was going to have to make sure I kept out of trouble for the foreseeable, or at least ensure I didn't get nicked. I chose the latter and pulled it off – just!

THE START OF IT!

I had been going to football with a friend called Colin; my brother was friends with his older brother, Martin. Colin was a tall, well-built lad, reaching six foot by the time we were 18. He had stopped me in the street some weeks earlier to introduce himself. He was a serial offender and had just been released from his latest term with Her Majesty. Over the years, Colin visited all forms of penal facilities the country had to offer, starting with the Detention Centres and Borstal, through to several terms in Dartmoor and Horfield prisons.

Our gang were either into or not into football, while two of them – Rich and Mark – were actually City fans. Probably another reason to start distancing myself. Unfortunately, it became 'out of the frying pan and into the fire'.

When you are around that age, so much happens in a short time that keeping track is an impossibility. During my time hanging around with Colin and before I joined the Army, we got up to several scrapes and misdemeanours, so much so that Colin was arrested for a deed that we had both been involved in. Colin went back to a young offenders' institute for a 10-month stretch. When the Police asked, 'Who helped you?', he said, 'I did it on my own; I made two trips.'

We had been on a little walkabout in Fishponds and opposite the Van Dyke bingo hall a light was on in a little sports shop. The Adidas t-shirt with the three stripes down the shoulder had become fashionable for the first time and there were a selection on display inside the shop. We both leant against the glass to have a little look. As we did, the door gave way a little: it hadn't been locked.

'Bloody hell, Col, we could nick one each!'

'Bugger that, we'll have the lot!' Colin answered.

As the lights were on and the Van Dyke was getting close to chucking out, we decided to go for a walk and return when it was quieter.

We just walked a few paces away towards the Full Moon pub and stopped by a pedestrian crossing. A couple of local lads rocked up and started angling for a row. We would have liked to accommodate them, but we had other plans for our evening. Just as we were finding it harder to resist the goading, a car pulled up and an off-duty policeman jumped out and scared the two lads off. Quick as a flash, we said, 'Thanks; we are waiting for our Mum to come out of the Bingo to walk her home.' He drove off and we decided to hunt down the two pricks that had attracted the attention of our friendly bobby.

Crossing the road and running in the direction they had left, we started scouring the side streets to catch a glimpse of them. Armed with a couple of bricks each, we gave chase quietly at first; and then, when we were in throwing distance, we launched our missiles at them with the customary, 'Come on then, you wankers!' or other such invitation.

The bricks landed close enough to stir our prey into running for all they were worth. We gave up the chase and returned to 'Plan A'.

We made our way back to the shop and were disappointed to see the lights had gone out. More in hope than anything, we tried the door. It was still open, so we dived in, hitting the floor as headlights from the traffic flooded the shop.

Colin immediately pulled several holdalls off the shelves and started scooping up the shirts, shoes, and anything else we could find. Darts and a little cash were found at the back, and with three bags each, we attempted to leg it across the Fishponds Road, up the side street past the Peckett Flyer pub and onto the most useful disused railway, all the way back to Easton. It took several attempts before the road was quiet enough to make our escape.

After hiding the spoils in Colin's father's attic, the next day we were modelling the very latest in sporty attire as we paraded around Eastville market taking orders. At the time I believe they were selling for around £5.99 and we were banging them out at £2 – bargain. All the lads on the market were keen on them and we flogged 25 before Colin's dad rumbled us and he grassed his son up. To be fair, Colin, when he was not serving time, was a one-man crime wave. This close shave was enough for me, and it was my last foray into this type of criminal activity.

As we got older, I always tried to make a trip to Dartmoor or Horfield prisons to visit him.

So, at 14, I travelled on the train to Plymouth for my first away game. The game was uneventful, but what a thrill walking back towards the station over Home Park in a huge army and the main boys, the Tote, grabbing the odd Argyle fan who strayed too close in the maelstrom of noise. A quick savage beating and then discarded from the swarming

THE START OF IT!

mass. I was in awe of these guys, and after getting a little fine for 'accidentally' breaking a light on the train, it was overall a great day out.

More star-struck times followed, notably an away game at Ashton Gate, home to the Shit (Bristol City), a fearsome rivalry at the time. In later years, the balance of power would shift, but then Bristol town centre was Blue. The Tote were kings. Meeting on the Centre, the shout would go to move off. It was then that the pubs began to spill out like fountains. Doc Marten-clad Skins and Boot Boys and Greasers swarmed onto the streets. Rovers were always an eclectic bunch, unique in many ways, no one style: if you were Blue, you were welcome. I was still a young 'un, as the older Bristol boys would call you, and with my mate Robert Michaels, we marched off the centre, through Prince Street and down the side of the river, swept along with the throng. As we got to the end of the pathway and started to climb the steps to cross the river over into Red country, I looked back and said to Rob, 'Christ, they're still coming onto the path!' Thousands of Rovers fans, an endless river of Blue, a sight I'll never forget.

In the ground, stood on the open end, you could feel the hatred for the red half of our great city. Any form of destruction was a good thing, and when the flagpole at the back of the Open End was snapped and clouted some poor lad on the head, the cheer was enormous; not, I hasten to add, for the lad that got brained by the pole. Half-time, an assault on the East End started. I was starting to climb the fence and a huge bloke behind asked, 'Are you going over?'

'Yeah,' I shouted, and he lifted myself and Rob up together to help us. We got over and raced towards their End. The charge was stopped by the law, but the die was cast. Some Tote Enders were already on the East End and my jealousy was palpable – you could see the two tribes facing off, as the Police tried in vain to cut short this vicious incursion. The excitement was intoxicating, I wanted more; but with summer approaching and ultimately Her Majesty the Queen's uniform after that, it would be some time before I felt the same rush of adrenaline.

Around the age of 15, my Mum suffered her first of three strokes. The third would eventually contribute to her passing away at 80 years of age, but the first struck her at the comparatively young mark of 45. It affected her right side and she became paralysed for a while, and as Dave was working, it fell on me to stay at home to care for her, a task I was, of course, pleased to do. I took over all the daily chores Mum did without thinking about it, and I learned quickly. Cooking, cleaning, laundry and ironing, all things that would stand me in good stead in the years to come. Around a month in, with Mum still bedridden, I received another patient. Dad was assisting in cleaning a skylight window at a business men's club managed by my Uncle Mervyn in the town centre. He put his leg through the glass, badly lacerating his knee and thigh. The workload increased, but I cared for them for around two months. Both made a full recovery, and I had collected some great life-skills.

FOR QUEEN AND COUNTRY

September 1976 raced around all too quickly: the hottest summer on record and a tan to prove it. I had spent the intervening months, after leaving school in May, working on the markets with a great trader called Clem, a sparkling row of gold teeth and smile to match. We had huge bacon butties with lashings of tomato sauce, washed down with the sweetest milky coffee from the world's biggest Thermos flask. He was a real character, who always treated me well.

We, of course, worked the old Eastville Market on Fridays and Sundays. It was in its heyday then, and the whole gang would work there for various stallholders. We had early starts, around 4 to 5am, in order to get the required tables and unload the stock, be it material, fruit and veg, or fashion (jeans) like Clem sold. If you were selected by the traders you would work all day and pack it all up at the end of the day. Clem drove a huge Mercedes van that had seen better days, and loading and unloading was a science, with a place for everything and all needing to be packed in a particular order. The van had an eight-track tape player and only one tape was ever played: Bob Marley and the Wailers, the music of choice for Clem. I never tired of it, though, and being from Easton, my tastes have always been for SKA music and Reggae.

It was good money back then. Saturdays in between the football season we worked Gloucester and Tuesdays at Caldicot. Loved it there, out earning and still only 15. The market site was right by a big comprehensive school, and me in my trendy jean waistcoat, no shirt, shocking long black hair and glorious tan – I thought I was the Dog's!!! 'The older I get, the better I was.'

Gloucester market was held in the Old Cattle market site, and one of the principal things you had to do while working these stalls was to keep an eye out for youngsters trying to nick something. Basically, anyone like yourself was worth watching. Clem had shooed off a couple of local boys and we kept a look-out for them as they patrolled the aisles. Clem spotted them as they approached an old lady, her wheelie shopping basket being pulled behind her much like the wagging tail of a puppy, her handbag draped over her left arm. We could both see the intention of these two delinquents, and as they approached her, Clem and I set off towards them. As soon as they went for the grab, we were on them. Clem held on to the old lady to prevent her falling, as I just bundled through these two juveniles, clipping one of them around the side of his head, and attempting to grab the other. Other traders immediately joined in, but they managed to wriggle free and run for all they were worth. You see, I was trying to be the good guy.

With August slipping into September, the glorious summer came to an end, and after a farewell party at The South Wales Railway Tavern, organised by Mum and Dad, with Uncles and Aunts, a few Cousins, Dave, of course, my girlfriend and most of the old gang, I was off to begin my career. The pub was a grimy little back-street boozer by the side of Stapleton Road Railway Station. It was Mum and Dad's local and was run by a family friend, where the cider and Southern Comfort flowed. Mum and Dad never showed much emotion, having survived many, many tough times throughout their childhoods and adult lives, but that evening I could see some pride in their eyes and a little sadness in Mum's.

Mum and Dad duly delivered me to the gates of Beachley Camp and I nervously waved them off. Just 16, and the first time away from home.

One of the shortest Army careers in history had begun.

Day One: enlistment. I signed in, with the Company Sergeant-Major casting his disapproving eye over the new intake. Smartly dressed by most standards, his wasn't most standards. After the booming rhetoric of 'You will become men,' blah, blah, 'I'm your mother now,' blah, 'The best decision you ever made,' 'Army this, Army that,' we were all marched off to the barber.

Now, as a committed recruit I had taken it on myself to have a little trim of my shoulder-length hair to show willing. Around eight at a time could squeeze into the 'shop' all in a row on flimsy metal cantilever chairs. As the shearing progressed, I felt the eyes of the 'Butcher' – sorry, Barber – on me. Of course, all the other cannon fodder had taken it upon themselves to have a real haircut. Stand up, shuffle along a seat, sit down. Repeat.

'I've been waiting for you,' he chuckled as I sat in his chair of misery.

'Just a bit off the sides and back, please,' I said, thinking this guy had a sense of humour. He didn't, and I wasn't laughing. He took the clippers and destroyed the right side all in one go. I now know where Phil Oakey got his Human League style from... ME!!

'Bet that feels lighter, doesn't it?' commented Chuckles. He ploughed on, raking up the back, and then the left got the same treatment. 'Next!' he shouted, leaving my big fringe at the front. I looked like I was walking backwards. Prick. 'You can tuck that lot under your beret,' he said. I was wrong: this bloke was a fucking comic genius.

Quartermaster store next for uniform. Now I've got a large head, so another opportunity for a piss-take. If I wanted to be in a *Carry On* film, I would have gone to stage school. 'Got a longer tape, Corporal?' was just one of the rib-busting comments. I'd only been there four hours and I already wanted to batter the Butcher and the Candlestick Maker. I hoped the bread with dinner was okay, or the Baker could have some, too.

We all got kitted out, then back to our barrack room. Sixteen to a room: actually not bad, with your own bed space and wardrobe. Out of our window I could see looming above us the Severn Bridge with all the cars racing out of Wales across the Rivers Wye and Severn to England. Out on that headland we were very exposed, and as autumn passed into winter, the wind and rain would hurtle up the Bristol Channel, freezing us to the bone.

Opposite me was a lad called Rob from Weston-Super-Mare. He was unpacking his suitcase and pulled out a long blue and white scarf. Joy! Another Rovers fan. Rob was a burly, broad lad and it looked like a good whack from him might smart a bit. We hit it off immediately: why wouldn't we when we shared the same passion? Of the other 14 in the room, we had fans of Bolton, Newcastle, Swansea and Man United, of course. Luckily, not a Shithead in sight.

We all proudly set about making our bed spaces our own by hanging the scarves and posters. Then we had a lesson in making a bed, regimental style. Bed packs are a way of folding your sheets and blankets into a nice oblong parcel, not unlike a wafer biscuit. Most of us got the hang of it, but we had one guy in our room who shouldn't have been anywhere near a uniform regime, and even further away from weapons.

Dougie Beesley had travelled up from his Dorset home on a Fantic moped. At the time this 50cc machine looked good, but needed a gear change every 50 yards or so. It really was a piece of crap.

He was so laid back, horizontal was his default position. He just never got the whole Army thing at all. When we had room inspections, he would always be picked up for something, be it dusty floor, shit locker, shit bed-making or his room job not up to scratch. We were all allocated weekly tasks in the dormitory to perform each day, in addition to ensuring your bed space was acceptable. This could be polishing the centre floor, cleaning the urinals or showers, or sweeping and polishing the corridor.

We all liked to join in the polishing floors because we just used to put one of the smaller lads into a blanket and sling it up and down. Brought the floor up a treat.

Dougie was a great lad, but just not with it. The consequences of him not working to standard meant quite often we were all punished with changing parades, where you were given two minutes to get into one dress code or another; this could go on for about five or six changes, and at the end, when everything was in disarray, you were then given 20 minutes for Regimental Locker inspection. This was where every bit of uniform, underwear, socks, suitcase, the lot, has to match a photo.

During the time in the room, we all discovered that different lads were better at some jobs than others, be it Ironing or bed-making. The guys that got the hang of bulling boots were invaluable. Polishing and buffing your dress boots for parades was usually outsourced to these guys, in my case in exchange for a bit of ironing, which I wasn't bad at, after my time as housekeeper looking after the parents.

The days started at around 5am: shower, shave (not too much to do there for most of us 16-year-olds), bed space job, room job before inspection, which allowed us to be released for breakfast.

Carrying your own issue mug and cutlery, you ran to the mess and queued. 'Wait there, you wankers!' shouted the head chef, a sergeant and a bruising beast of a man.

To be fair, the food there was very good and we never went short.

After that, depending on the day, you then either went to your designated classes for your trade, or physical training. As apprentices, we did our classes during the mornings and for a while after lunch, and then spent some time in the gym or out running. Saturday mornings were reserved for Military Training, where we would be put through our paces on the parade square or sent off to the ranges for arms training.

After a couple of weeks, we started to get fitness testing and targets issued for improvements, and also given chances to play a variety of sports. We were all marched down to watch a college rugby match against some opposition from the police or navy. 'We think you might be able to play hooker; what do think?' said one of the Physical Training Instructors (PTI).

I deferred my reply until after I'd watched the match. I was always more into football anyway, and after witnessing the utter carnage on the pitch involving broken bones and ripped-up Coke cans being flashed up into faces in the scrum, I declined the offer, asking, 'What else have you got?'

Next up was a trip to the gym for a bit of boxing. Now we're talking! Many years ago, my Dad had been a well-respected amateur boxer, and this got me excited. I reasoned that there would only be one hitting me instead of 15 – much better odds.

The PTI called out pairings to get in the ring and have a go. I was matched with a lad from our room, a tough lad from Porthcawl, who was actually already the junior Army Judo Champion. The PTI shouted 'Fight!', and we went at it with absolutely no finesse. Judo boy Graham caught me square on the jaw and really rattled me, so, without thinking, I kneed him in the groin and he dropped to his knees.

'Stop fighting!' shouted the Instructor.

'Bollocks,' I thought, 'I'm in the crap now.'

'You're aggressive, you're in the team!' shouted the PTI to me.

I apologised to Graham and he was okay about it, although later that evening, messing about, he got me in a headlock and I thought my head was going to burst like a melon. He said after he was relieved, as he had enough on with his judo commitments. I think he had serious ambitions to take it as far as he could.

THE GOOD AND THE BAD

Things seemed to be going well for me in the Army. My apprenticeship had begun, and initially I was working on a forge doing a short smithy class. I still have a cold chisel I made way back then. The boxing was great; I had already had a couple of victories, stopping both opponents. We'd been to Weymouth and did a course on Chesil Beach making rafts and generally arsing about in the sea. We had a trip coming up in the Brecon Beacons involving a hike to Pen-Y-Fan. Rob and I had even managed to get to a couple of home games. As I said, we used to do our Military Training on a Saturday morning and be able to get off at 12 noon, as long as all went well; so we concentrated and asked the guys not to fuck it up today. Our Sergeant at the time was a tough Scotsman who I really liked and he knew when we wanted to get off, having said that he would tease us until the last minute; but he dismissed the parade in time for Rob and I to run to our room, get washed and changed, and run to the guardhouse to check out. A bus used to stop outside the camp, but we would never have the patience to wait for it.

We'd then run the three miles or so into Chepstow, always in time to jump aboard the bus to Bristol. 55p one way – we never bothered with a return because, after tea at Mum's, Dad would always drop us back.

The bus would be heading for the station near the Bear Pit, and if we were early we'd travel all the way. Often, though, we would get off at the top of Muller Road and run all the way to Eastville. If I had to do that much running now, I'd never see a game. Would have been fine now, though, with the Memorial Stadium at the top of Muller Road.

Beachley was, in fact, a glorified college, the purpose being to turn spotty youths into trained, skilled soldiers. The apprenticeships would last for two years. Every term you progressed through the establishment, starting as PIGs (Passing In Group) and finishing the second year as the POGs (Passing Out Group). They were also known as senior group, and it was their 'duty' to make the PIGs as uncomfortable as possible. Senior group's final week was always held in trepidation by the younger intakes waiting for the inevitable midnight raids on the room. This was the week when the seniors had finished their training and were Passing Out into the Regular Army. When you made it into the later terms, promotions were available, and the better leaders were given ranks up to Apprentice Sergeant. These senior leaders would use that additional clout to menace the new intake. One night, we were raided and I woke to see Apprentice Sergeant Crabtree, a tall, growling Scotsman, jumping up and down on the base of my bed. Without thinking, I rolled over as he was landing. As my legs had changed position, he lost his landing spot and his feet were wiped out beneath him. He instantly collapsed off the bed, banging his head in the process. He leapt to his feet and immediately tipped the bed from the side, cascading me to the floor in a cocoon of sheets and blankets. Some of the others in the room, though, received sentry boxes: this is where the bed is still tipped up, only from the base upright against the wall, leaving the unfortunate occupant pinned and crumpled inside. Another lad in our room, Geordie March, was getting 'smothered' by another senior group arsehole with his own pillow, with the assailant shouting, 'Don't resist, don't resist!'

The Durham lad pulled the pillow down and puffed out, shouting, 'I might be green, but I'm not a fucking cabbage!'

Even while trying to extricate myself from the bedding, I found it hilarious. Another favourite of the senior group on their midnight raids was to get everyone up and out of bed, marched out of the rooms and onto the Ponderosa. This was a name given to a large grassed area with diagonal paths crossing from the corners. No time was given to get dressed; we were just bundled out as we were, whatever the weather. Mess tins were strapped to you around the waist, front and back, and then you were ordered to complete three laps running. The clanging of the tins sounded like a stampede on an Austrian dairy farm.

During the trip to the Brecon Beacons, we all had to take turns through the night on guard duty. Three at a time, armed with a torch, whistle and pickaxe handle. One would stay on the gate, while the other two patrolled the perimeter fence. In the pitch black this was an opportunity too good to miss for the Apprentice Corporals, jumping out from behind bushes to frighten the young soldiers. The antics stopped halfway through the night, though, as Apprentice Corporal Crompton leapt out on one of the lads who hailed from Clacton. Instantly, rather than jump, he swung his pickaxe handle, catching Crompton across the upper arm right where his soon-to-be-removed stripes were, breaking his arm.

The next day our actual regular Sergeant congratulated us on our night's patrol, adding just one criticism. He commented that the whole camp appeared to be lit up like Blackpool Illuminations with the torches that were only meant to be used to identify an intruder.

We then had the main exercise of the trip to complete, which involved a hike from the camp with Bergens and weapons. At the time the Army were still using the SLR, a rifle they had been using for decades and a decent bit of kit which weighed around four or five kilograms. The object was to map-read to two points: one an obelisk dedicated to a young boy that had perished on these bleak wind-swept hills, and then on to Pen-y-Fan, the highest point on the Brecon Beacons, then back to camp. During this we also had to cook a meal in the field using the little burners and field rations. All very exciting for us young soldiers. The weather was horrendous, with the wind and snow flurries driving horizontally across the wilderness. Sheep were grazing everywhere and appeared on the most inaccessible outcrops. We were struggling up and down the inclines, slipping on loose rocks and wet grass. Occasionally, a fog would descend on us and we would have no option but to huddle down and drape ourselves in our green-issue ponchos, as visibility became no more than around 10 foot. As we reached the summit of Pen-Y-Fan, another dense cloud descended on us. No alternative: we once again wrapped up and sat against the monument and waited for the murk to lift. Visibility started to improve, and in the distance along a long ridge we noticed five silhouettes running towards us. As they got closer and the fog continued to lift, we could see them all dressed in black with huge Bergens easily three times the weight of ours, and these guys were running!!! We all stood as they got to us and we instantly recognised them as Special Forces. They looked at us and were more than kind enough to acknowledge our Royal Engineer cap badges, passing compliments before continuing their morning stroll. To say we were impressed is an understatement, and it encouraged us to crack on with the exercise. We finished the hike second of six patrols and again received the congratulations of our Sergeant.

One wet and windy morning, we were taken out to the marsh around the headland. Another boy soldier training exercise: camouflage and concealment. A small group of us were instructed to disappear into the marsh and, using foliage to disguise the outline of our helmets, we then had to conceal ourselves and wait until we were found. With the camo crème slavered on our faces, we split up and melted into the undergrowth.

I got myself well tucked away against a short hedgerow and hunkered down with a beady eye keeping a lookout all around. After around 20 minutes, I heard our Sergeant shout, although I didn't catch what was being said, so I stayed put. Around 15 minutes later I decided to have a crafty look towards our RV (rendezvous point). I couldn't see anyone, so I crept along the hedgerow to a larger tree line. From there I got a better view and could see absolutely no one. They had all fucked off!! Still stupidly staying in cover, I crept to the meeting point. Sure enough, not a soul there; just me, all camouflaged up and feeling like a prize dick. I doubled round to the company office and as I rounded the corner I was met with a huge cheer. I was promptly escorted by a guard of four and marched to the Armoury to check in my rifle. Apparently, the call from our Sergeant was for us all to stand and reveal ourselves and then come in. Over an hour and a half I was hidden in the damp bog.

Once a month a trip was organised on a Thursday to The Silver Blades Ice Rink in Bristol. I'd leapt at the chance to get back home for a couple of hours, made even better by meeting my girlfriend at the time. Sue Richards was a gorgeous girl and in hindsight I was definitely punching above my weight. 'The older I get, the better I was.' There it is again.

Sitting on the coach on the way back, an Apprentice Corporal, who was a year above us, couldn't believe I'd pulled when he had struck out. 'Well, I'm from Bristle in I, an' I talks creck Bristle, mind.' Never had the heart to tell him the truth, and he didn't have a clue I was taking the piss.

Unfortunately, it was trips like this that brought home how much I was missing home, even though before too long she would pack me in because I wasn't there.

Other incidents started to happen, which, of course, always got back to our commanding officers and staff. As we had all settled down into the routine of living together, some friction inevitably crept in.

I have never been the tallest, no more than 5ft 6in when in the Army and only some two inches taller now. But despite my lack of stature and being exceedingly fit back then, I still weighed around 10st. Again, I'm quite a bit more than that now. However, the consequence of my disproportionate height-to-weight ratio meant that the majority of my boxing bouts were against much taller beanpole types.

I don't think I possess a 'small man's syndrome', but I have definitely got an 'I don't give a fuck who you are' attitude.

The following two events are examples. Messing about in our room, one of the lads, a 6ft 2in basketball player, grabbed me by my rather fetching cardigan, causing a little tear. Immediately I attacked, knocking him back so he stumbled over a bed and flapped in a vain effort to protect himself. It was an instinctive reaction, but looking back, was it the same reaction my old mate Rob Michaels had with his jumper goalpost? I was pulled back and I calmed down remarkably quickly. I get several strange looks from the other lads, but Rob put his arm around me and took me to our part of the room. The lanky twat put his notice in a week later and left.

The second incident happened a week or so later. We were marching in a platoon, dressed in football kit and boots, with the Army-issue 'flasher macs' as protection against the rain lashing down at us. We were on our way, obviously, to play football. As one of the shorter members of the troop, I was middle row of three and centre area from front to back. In front of me was another tall gangly lad from somewhere up north, with big prominent bony features, and he was an all-round cocky arsehole. For some reason he stopped marching; I assumed his lace may be untied, but all the same, you don't stop while marching. I gave him a push to get him going, but he stopped again, pushing his backside back hard. I reached forward with both hands on his left side and threw him from the group. I attempted to carry on regardless, but I then heard the sound of his football boots running to get back in line. My timing was so precise: as the clip-clop got close, I spun around and threw what still today I feel was the best straight left-hand drive fully into his face. The punch connected just below his giant bony nose, causing it to tear away on both sides. He fell back, clutching the ragged edges of his wound, trying to stem the not insignificant flow of blood.

My lovely Sergeant had witnessed the whole thing and. bellowing my name, he shouted, 'Get your fucking arse out here, you little wanker!'

Football was cancelled for me that day and I think we lost another recruit after some eight stiches were embroidered into his ugly mug. Well, ugly now for sure.

***

The two incidents, along with a couple of other minor faults, were reported and I found myself in front of the Captain. When he said, 'You're not quite fitting in, are you?', it reminded me of Goldie Hawn in *Private Benjamin*. Shall I say, 'It will be okay when you all come round to my way of thinking'?

It seemed I was in the ridiculous position of being a little too violent for the British Army!!!

Next thing, our delightfully understanding Sergeant was moved on and was replaced by a 20-year cockney veteran. The dislike was instant and mutual. I just hated this fucker, and I think his arrogance was the reason why.

The end of my military career was looming fast. Firstly, I suffered a perforated eardrum during boxing training and had to medically withdraw from the college finals. Also, the girlfriend had packed me in. I always seemed to get the shit jobs on room duty. Urinals or toilets or both, courtesy of the swaggering Sergeant. I think it annoyed the hell out of him, though, as I took all the crap and smiled through gritted teeth. The final death knell came one morning. We were on bed packs for room inspection and Dougie had typically just left his bed covered in blankets. The Sergeant bawled, 'What is this?'

I was stood in front of him next to Rob, looking directly at the dishevelled bed space of our spaced-out room-mate. I just leaned over to Rob and whispered, 'That's Beesley.' Next thing I felt was a sharp whack on my shoulder from the Sergeant's pace stick, a device carried to measure a marching stride. Not a second thought at 5.30 in the morning, and I spun and threw a punch. Big, big mistake. In the first place, it wasn't a patch on the peach I had launched in the rain, and secondly, this was not a gangly 16-year-old. A barrage came back. I seem to remember I had an out-of-body experience. I had peripheral vision and could see all my colleagues diving for cover as I went sailing past. His experience told, as he was careful to generally keep the blows landing in non-bruising areas. He had a degree of success. I didn't bow down, though, but I did stop reacting. Why prolong the slaughter? I thought.

After being escorted to the guardhouse for a day or two, my next meeting with the Officer class had been upgraded. I was now in front of Major Ring and the Regimental Sergeant-Major, amongst others. The concerns were raised again about my poor discipline. It was late January, and I was almost five months in. As a boy soldier we were given six months to decide if this was the life we wanted. I made the decision to leave there and then. I'm sure the assembled panel were relieved.

This short career had at least given me some training. I was so fit I looked ill, drawn and thin. I had reinforced the knowledge that I would stand my ground if and when it was needed, and my confidence was boosted immensely.

So, two weeks later, I was back on Civvy Street, wondering what I was going to do now.

ROVERS EVERYWHERE

It took me three weeks to find a job. I'd enjoyed the trade I had been learning, so was keen to continue in an engineering-type environment. I started work for a firm, making office furniture, amongst other things, in Fishponds.

'We'll start you on the production line and every few months we will move you around the departments,' said the foreman, as I was given a tour of the cavernous factory. Sounded like just what I needed. There were some 400 people in all working there within various departments. The whole place was divided into two factories, 'A' and 'B'. 'A' factory was where all the wood production took place. We never had a lot to do with that end of the site, other than when we needed materials to make our own bookcases or shelves for home. We would get really pally with them then. Our domain in 'B' factory covered such departments as Machine Shop, Detail, Tool Room, Plastics, Shop-fitting, Upholstery, Paint Shop, Treatment, Dispatch, and, of course, Assembly. There were several young lads working there, mainly from the local Hillfields, Oldbury Court and Kingswood areas, and almost to a man these guys were Rovers fans. The Kingswood lads particularly I got to know well, travelling to games with them and, of course, standing on the Tote End.

Bristol Rovers have never experienced real success, but the fan-base is surprisingly large. On the rare occasions we have played in play-off finals or lower league cup final games, the support – be it at Wembley or the Millennium Stadium – has always been staggering. We also travel in great numbers to our games; in relation to our home games, the percentage of away travelling fans is impressive.

It seems wherever I have been, anywhere at all, I always run into a Rovers fan. During the Euros in 2018, I was on holiday in a place called Moraira, Costa Blanca North. We found a seat in the square to watch an England game and started to chat to a lad in front of us. I knew the area very well and he said he'd been living up the road in Benitchatell for some years. His accent was familiar and he said he used to live in Bedminster, so my interest waned as I thought he had to be a Shithead!! But no. Straight away he pulled up his sleeve to reveal a tattoo, scrawled with the words, 'I'll see you in my dreams'. The words belong to the song *Goodnight Irene*, sung by Rovers fans for decades and synonymous with us, much like *Bubbles* is for West Ham, or *Blue Moon* at Manchester City.

During our year languishing in the Conference, I had an enormously good feeling the day Rovers were playing away in Essex at Braintree Town. My wife and I had met a couple, Martin and Michelle, from Braintree whilst on holiday a couple of years earlier in Cape Verde and remain great friends, taking several holidays together and visiting each other regularly.

I arranged for us to go up and stay the weekend of the game with them. My wife stayed at our friends' house with Michelle, enjoying their wonderful garden and a bottle or two of wine, whilst Martin and I, along with a couple of other friends of his, made our way to the football. We stopped at his local pub, 'The Orange Tree', before the game. On the walk down, I was recognised by several Rovers lads, all shouting out. Martin couldn't get over the fact we were in his home town and I knew more people than he did. ROVERS EVERYWHERE. You may not know all their names, but you know the faces.

LEARNING CURVE

With my Army 'career' over, I no longer had to worry about behaving myself. I was back living at home, able to get served in the pub and football every weekend. All I needed for a while.

Still a juvenile, and a home game against Nottingham Forest. A full Tote End, and boisterous as ever. At the time as a young 'un, we would stand under the main shed behind the goal and sing ourselves hoarse. The Police had made an incursion onto the terrace and were trying to apprehend someone; the good old Hokey Cokey started up and a rush into the arresting officers released their prey and all manner of articles, including a helmet, were catapulted into the air. The sway and push of the crowd carried us all around as if on a tidal wave, and the poor helmet suffered a severe stomping, making it almost unrecognisable. Not deliberately, I was one of the stompers, and as the tide receded I got singled out as the culprit. Looking over my shoulder, I noticed the long arm of the law reaching out towards me. First reaction: leg it. I moved away and then ducked and changed direction just in time to see one of the thin blue line fly overhead. Unfortunately, my next evasive manoeuvre was not as successful, and I was trapped by two other of Avon and Somerset's finest and was wrestled to the ground to the sound of, 'Got you, you little fucker.' I, of course, protested my innocence as the three of them carted me off to the lock-up cell at the end of the old wooden stand.

This was my first arrest at football, aside from the broken light on the train coming back from Plymouth, and I didn't know if, as was sometimes the case, I would just be kicked out at the end of the game. As was usual around then, there were several Rovers fans in there, none of which seemed to have a care in the world other than asking who had scored when a huge roar went up outside. With all of us with nylon straps tied to the round rings on the wall, it reminded me of a bus stop. One by one we were all processed: nice photo with the arresting officer, with some of the comedians asking if the photographer could get his best side, or, 'Can I comb my hair?' I didn't think to ask if I could have a group photo with all three of the officers that had apprehended me. It then dawned on me that someone was going to pay for the damage to the policeman's helmet as I, along with a few others, were loaded onto a van and transported to Lockleaze Police Station. As a 16-year-old, I was slammed into a cell and had to wait for Dad to come and get me after being interviewed and charged. I now started to worry a bit as I remembered the most telling punch I had ever received. Luckily, Dad arrived with one of my favourite Uncles, who was Mum's youngest brother, and while Dad made the right noises to the officers, I had time with my Uncle there to give my account of the event. It went to juvenile court and I was represented by a barrister as a favour to Uncle Mervyn, who managed the businessmen's club mentioned earlier. A bit like taking a sledgehammer to crack a nut, but, hey, who was I to complain. The whole affair was laughable, with the helmet being held up in court as exhibit 'A' – and a sorry state it looked. Multiple boot marks, strangely all with the Doctor Marten sole print, the badge detached on one side, with the rivet having pulled straight through the material, leaving a jagged hole, and the shiny top cap almost crushed flat.

The magistrate decided I was guilty and would have to pay for the replacement, along with a punitive fine. The magistrate then asked how much the item cost. Nobody seemed to know, and my lawyer stood up and commented that the helmet must be priceless. We then have to hang around while they send for someone from the stores to come over, swear an oath and declare that the helmet cost £15. This was 1977, after all, and with the £5 fine, taking into account my low wages and no previous record, I asked for time to pay at the rate of £1 a week. This was agreed and the hilarity stopped as I was released.

Another away day, to Orient on a Tote End coach. In reality, most of us were still kids, but under the Skull and Crossbones banner we thought we were the dogs. Pride before a fall, I've heard before. It happened that day.

The coach we travelled on was not a luxury model; in fact, it could have come straight out of a 1950s black and white *Carry On* movie. Off we set to London. City at this time were lauding it up in the First Division and were at home to West Ham United. Sounds great, but I wouldn't swap places. Rovers or nothing for me.

We pulled into the services for a comfort break and we all piled out to stretch our legs. Suddenly, someone shouted, 'Everybody on the coach now!!'

Looking out across the motorway, I spotted several huge donkey jacket-clad objects. I may be wrong, but at the time they seemed to be running straight across the road, and I swore they were stopping traffic with their outstretched shovel-sized hands.

I got on and raced to the back seat, where another friend, Nigel, was sitting with his girlfriend Mandy. Nigel was a modern-day hippie, the drummer in a local punk band, but so like Neil from *The Young Ones* it was uncanny. I had got to know him only recently as Nigel's Dad, who was a hard-drinking, spiky Scotsman, had taken over our local pub, the Queens Head on Easton Road.

As the driver attempted to pull away, the last to board the coach was still in the doorway: a small lad with glasses, known then as Joe 90. A large arm wrapped around his face and attempted to yank him from safety, fortunately failing. Then, on the motorway side of the coach, two large windows were shattered as great lumps of rock were launched at the fleeing 'school' bus. I looked out of the back window and saw another 'Cockney Geezer' setting to throw another rock. Instinctively, I dived lengthways across the back seat onto Mandy. The missile luckily bounced off the window.

'Is everyone here?' shouted the organiser.

'I am!' some Smart Alec chimed in.

'No!' shouted someone else. We looked out of the back window to see the remaining Tote Ender galloping for all he was worth down the slip road to the motorway.

We managed to keep the windows in for quite some time, and someone had a huge Union Jack flag, which doubled up as a very useful tent.

On entering the ground, our mood had changed to one of some sort of revenge. Brisbane Road, home to Leyton Orient, was at the time similar to many of the grounds in the lower echelons of the league:

decrepit, run-down shells of the temples they had been intended to be when constructed. During the late 1970s, some of these stadiums were soulless places haunted by past glories, long disappeared behind the cold concrete steps and damp mouldy buildings. The VIPs lived it up in probably the only room with any modicum of comfort or, dare I say, luxury, while the rank and file slummed it on the litter-strewn terraces.

We spotted a few lads, obviously not Bristol Boys by the way they dressed, nor was it likely they were Orient fans, mainly because they didn't have any. 'Got to be West Ham' – the most local team to where we were. The terrace was sparsely populated, so we were able to make a straight charge at them. 'BARRISTOL, BARRISTOL!' the chant went as we all targeted our prey. In later years, we'd learn the art of patience and subterfuge as a better method of engaging the enemy. These few lads heard us and were off like rockets, down the terrace and onto the pitch and away.

As young 'kiddies' around that time, the majority of these events involved a lot of shouting, singing and running, with very little actual fighting. I soon tired of this and looked for more.

Later that season we took another trip, this time to Blackpool, the furthest I'd travelled, and Nigel came with me. We didn't manage to get on the main Tote coaches, so travelled on a Supporters' Club coach. Not a patch on the craic we could have with the others, but at least we were going. We arrived at this massive coach park in the shadow of the ground. Our instructions were: straight back to the coach after the game. We went to the game and I remember feeling immensely jealous as the vast majority of Rovers fans made a bee-line for the beach when we left the stadium. We trudged over to the far side of the coach park to our transport. A few of us were stood around, waiting for the rest to arrive, breathing in our last gulps of sea air before the long journey back south. With the coach behind us, on the right was a chain-mesh fence leading away and out of the coach park; in the same direction to the left, there seemed to be a double-storey car park. It was from here that a rampaging mob of around 30 Blackpool fans came hurtling towards us.

'I never thought to run, when perhaps I should have. Now I couldn't run if I wanted to!' I stood my ground, along with another two of us. One, a taller lad, I didn't know, but fair play to him for standing with us, and another who I did recognise: he went by a nickname, 'Nobby', and hailed from Knowle West. Must be handy supporting Rovers and living there, I thought, and so it proved to be the case.

'Don't run!' Nobby shouted. Never crossed my mind, I thought. The horde of screaming banshees were closing on us and we stayed put. They got closer and started to slow down. I could see the expressions on their faces changing – it was a picture, and they just didn't seem to understand why we weren't running. This was more of what I'd been looking for.

In a comic twist, they actually stopped within about six feet of us and looked rather perplexed. I bet they had never seen the like: we were outnumbered 10 to 1 and stood there ready. The uneasy silence was broken by Nobby basically encouraging them to do something, but they just didn't seem to want to react, until their 'leader' offered a limp kick in Nobby's direction. That was the trigger. I dived in and landed a decent blow across his gormless face. At last it kicked off; that was the starting pistol for them, and they decided to join in. The hits were coming thick and fast and I just kept on pumping the punches out. I could feel kicks and fists landing almost everywhere, but luckily the size of the mob meant that not all were landing cleanly. I consoled myself that every time I hit something it had to be one of them. I drove myself into the mob and got myself up against the mesh fence. It seemed like a good plan, as presumably I couldn't get attacked from behind. It was then that I seemed to become the centre of attention. Through the melee I could see my mate Nigel; as I said, he was a modern-day hippie, and his jaw was wide open, not having a clue what to do. To be honest, a little bit of assistance would have been appreciated, but I was still having a ball. Way back then, as young 'uns, we often wore a scarf. When I entered this fray, I made a point to tie it around my waist. Some little ratty fucker got in low and started tugging away. I tried to swing my right elbow, but it just glanced off him. As the bombardment continued, the fence prevented me from going down, so the master plan was working! I was just bouncing back into further punishment. The determined ratty worked the scarf loose and then, like a single entity, they broke off and ran for the multi-storey. I was seething and started to run after them, but was a little knackered, to say the least, and realised it was a futile thing to attempt. Not for the first time or the last, I felt the rush that comes with the territory and felt my senses heighten with the thrill of it all.

We boarded the coach high on adrenaline and basked in the glory. Nigel was apologetic and more than once questioned my sanity. The next day I literally could not get out of bed. I had multiple bruises and scratches, but I didn't care at all; it even hurt to smile, but I couldn't stop.

As I said, Nigel was a drummer when we were young and he continued on that path, taking a detour via Japan, where he married, and now tours performing the Japanese art of drumming. In 2019, my wife and I went to see him perform not too far from where we live. He hadn't met her before and the first words to her were, 'He's a nutter!' Nice to have made an impression.

BACK ON MY BACK

Unfortunately, in November that year, 1977, I was forced to take another break from my beloved Bristol Rovers and my blossoming career on the terraces.

Friday night, and I had just moved departments at work. At last away from the mundane assembly line, I had moved to the Detail Shop, where great big 200-tonne presses grinded away in a slow demonic wail. The guys that worked there had slaved away at the same job for years and years, and some of them carried the trophies of times when safety wasn't a priority. Missing fingers were common in the boiler suit-clad brigade. I was excited to be in this shop, not for the towering monster presses, but the welding booths were here also. This was where I wanted to work. Tommy the comical foreman came up and asked how I was. He was a lovely, slightly bow-legged man who walked with a swaggering gait, and the thumb hooked into the pocket of his trousers only increased the Chaplin-style walk. His thick-rimmed glasses masked a very kind face. We all liked Tommy, but that said, he was good for us lads, who would constantly take advantage of his good nature.

'Fancy some overtime tomorrow, lad?'

'Yes, sure, Tommy, I'll be here.'

Well, at 17, a little thing like work in the morning wasn't stopping my weekend. Out for a few drinks with Rich and Marcus, all on our mopeds: mine was a Suzuki SP50 and they both had the Yamaha FS1E, or Fizzy as they were commonly called.

We headed for town and settled on the Naval Volunteer in King Street. The Volunteer was an ancient building on this historic cobbled street, which is home to many bars, restaurants and the famous Old Vic Theatre. Further up there is now a T-junction; originally the road carried on towards the waterfront of Welsh Back. On this crossroads are two other notable pubs. On the left, the Old Duke is famous for jazz music, and opposite is the Llandoger Trow pub, mentioned in *Treasure Island* under the name Admiral Benbow and reportedly the place where Daniel Defoe met Alexander Selkirk, the inspiration for *Robinson Crusoe*.

We had a couple or four and set off to be closer to home. This November night had not been too cold, but it had started to rain a little and the wind had got up considerably. We were all dressed for a night out, but not really for riding motorbikes. I personally had on a pair of jeans, a cotton shirt and a cardigan, which had very briefly become fashionable again.

We rode up the shiny wet cobbles of King Street towards the junction, which was very busy with cars parked fully up to the corners, the pubs opposite filling up with Friday night revellers. I was at the front and braked before moving out and around the cars. The view to the right was slightly blind and I didn't see the large car moving at '30mph'. More importantly, the driver didn't see me until it was too late. The last recollection I had before the impact was of a set of headlights and thinking, 'This is going to really hurt.'

The car hit me full in the side and then collided with four other parked cars. In the meantime, I managed to achieve unpowered flight for the second time in my life, as I sailed over a car parked on the near side of the road to me. I finished up on the pavement some 50 yards from the impact. My bike was a mess, and so was I.

The driver got out of his car, shouting out it was my fault, just in time for Rich to crack him around the head with a well-timed punch. Rich stabbing me in the leg is properly forgiven now.

Marcus ordered Rich to get to my house to tell my parents. Probably a good move, as who knows what he would have done to the driver next. The pub called for an ambulance – no mobile phones back then, of course.

I woke up in the Bristol Royal Infirmary: I had sustained several broken bones. Kneecap, thigh in two places, wrist and both bones in my forearm, as well as my elbow being completely shattered. I spent three weeks in the BRI and then over three months in Winford Orthopaedic Hospital, out in the country the wrong side of Bristol. Not the Christmas I had planned for. During my time in hospital I underwent general anaesthetic six times. I was told that the surgeons initially thought about removing my arm above the elbow because they didn't believe I would regain the use of my hand. To be fair, it did take around three months before I did. The problem was that when an arm is broken like mine was, the radial nerve was also severed, and it was a waiting game for it to re-grow, if at all. At least Dave and I became closer as a result of this. Probably just as well – I would never have beaten him with one arm. I also hope the hospital forgave me for the several glass tumblers I launched across the ward in an effort to open my hand and grasp them.

The first few days in the BRI were a foggy haze. Incomplete visions of nurses arriving at my bedside and harpooning my thigh with painkillers. After a few days, though, the pain was brought under control. I had been through the first couple of surgeries and was able to survey my surroundings.

I found myself in a ward of six beds. I was against the outside wall, with windows either side of me. One bed to my left and two to my right. In front, at a ninety degree angle, were the other two. Straight in front was the door, and to the right a large glass window with the nurses' station visible through that. A couple of the patients that were in the ward with me were somewhat unwanted celebrities, hitting the headlines at the time. Firstly, and rather tragically, next to me on my left was a security guard who had been travelling in the back of a security van which had skidded in the poor weather, lost control and plummeted off the Cumberland Basin. The vehicle landed on its roof onto a small man-made island.

The best part of a quarter of a million pounds in coin fell onto this unfortunate man's chest, crushing him in the process. He was extremely poorly and I did my best to lift his spirits when he asked most mornings how he looked.

The other was a young boy around 14 or 15 who had visited Bristol Zoo. This was shortly after the brand new reptile house experience had opened. The new attraction had walkways and a bridge that crossed the crocodile 'river'. The new patient had leant over the bridge, just far enough for one of the crocs to reach his arm. It leapt out of the water and took a significant bite.

The repercussions for the Zoo must have been horrendous, and as such there were two very attractive female employees stationed at his bedside, pandering to his every request. Of course, all of the other patients kept asking them for crocodile sandwiches, and to make them snappy. And most evenings, when the girls left, a short rendition of 'See you later, alligator' rang out around the ward.

A few days before I was moved, I had the chance to get a good look at my damaged arm. The nurses arrived along with the surgeon to inspect and re-dress the forearm that had had a plate fitted. As they started the big reveal, slowly unwrapping the bandaging and starting from the wrist, the raw wound started to show itself. At each turn, the wound just went on and on. The skin had not had much time to start healing and was just two scabby sides butted together with stitch after stitch. It seemed to go on and on, and as it reached the elbow it then deviated off for a few inches more. This was obviously what created the flap for access. I had only had a couple of operations at the time and it became apparent that more work was needed as my elbow was a strange swollen shape and in totally the wrong place.

As a 17-year-old, it was quite a shock, but I listened to the doctor and remained calm. At least it was still attached.

In order to be transferred to the other hospital at Winford, my leg was lashed up like Gulliver in Lilliput and I was wheeled to a waiting ambulance.

Winford Hospital was a former camp for Canadian troops during the war, and it felt like it. The wards were all separate singular buildings, long and plain as a barrack would be. They were all connected by a long sloping corridor that followed the hill that it was built on. All the windows were still metal-framed – no double glazing here – and although I'm sure the whole place was painted a hue of magnolia, no wall appeared to be the same shade as another. Operating theatres were on another part completely to the wards, and when patients had to go for various procedures they were collected in a whining electric vehicle. It had the appearance of a converted milk float. The winter of '77 to '78 was bitterly cold, and around January we were actually snowed in. Typically, the snow fell on a Friday night and the majority of the nursing staff were partying it up in central Bristol. The remaining nurses and domestics did a sterling job feeding us breakfast, which consisted of the most brittle piece of toast and an egg with the consistency of a super ball.

Being in an orthopaedic hospital had its advantages. We mainly all had broken bones of varying severity, so there was a slack attitude to drinking. I, for instance, always had at least two flagons of Natch cider and a bottle of Southern Comfort in my locker. As Christmas approached, as many of the patients as possible were discharged to go home. The remainder were all compressed into other wards. It meant in our ward all the younger boys were at the far end near the TV. They really packed us in so much that the bed next to mine, occupied by a nice lad called Duncan, who had broken his left leg, was no more than 18 inches from me. One evening around then, we had been drinking quite a bit and Duncan fell out of bed into the gap between us. We were both on traction with our legs pinned and strung up to a weight to hold the bones in position. He managed to touch the floor with his hand, while his broken leg flew into the air. I reached over and cupped his head with my left arm, as it was my right arm and leg that were broken. This caused my right leg to jut out to my left and he managed to entangle his good leg into his hand grip above his head. It was the strangest game of Twister ever witnessed.

We used to find things to do to keep amused, other than reading or watching television. One of the ways to pass the time was to see how many Maltesers you could stuff in your mouth. Sounds banal, I know, but when you are confined to a bed for weeks and weeks on end, the smallest daft things can be very amusing. But our favourite game was to drink as much as possible and the winner was the one who could fill the bottle nearest to the top. The nurses weren't that keen on that game, as we used to manage close to 10mm from the rim. More than once we heard the crash of overfilled piss bottles scattering onto the floor of the sluice room. Another lad had a penchant for peanuts, and whenever he ordered a bed pan we asked the nurses to bring a metal one. You would have thought he had a machine gun in there when using it.

During my time in there, my joke of a court appearance reared its head as a warrant for my arrest was issued, as I had defaulted on my payment plan.

'Let them try and get me,' I said, as I lay there trussed up like a fly caught in a spider's web.

As I had been in hospital for a while not spending money, I wrote a cheque for £10 and paid the balance. Flashy or what?

The months dragged by and eventually I was told I could go home. The problem was my thigh had been broken high on my leg and had still not healed sufficiently. So a plaster called a Hip Spiker was fitted. This is a plaster from the chest to the ankle, and very uncomfortable to wear.

Before it could be fitted, I had to have the pins removed from my kneecap. This was done while I was still in the ward with no more than some local anaesthetic, a scalpel and a pair of pliers. Nothing was simple with me, and the nurse and training doctor checked the X-ray and skilfully cut the skin and located the first pin. A good uncomfortable tug and the piece of surgical steel slid through the bone and was plonked into a kidney dish. One down, one to go. A little cut to reveal the bent end of the wire, and after getting a good grip with the pliers, a nice tug. This time, though, the kneecap didn't give up the pin, and the pain was not insignificant. The carry-on doctor decided to 'carry on', and had another go without success. The nurse suggested looking at the X-ray again, and they discovered that the pin had been folded over at both ends. Genius. Our Junior Doctor then attempted to straighten the exposed end, then realised he didn't have enough anaesthetic to cut the other side, his plan being to yank it out the other end. Off he trotted for more supplies, leaving me and the nurse staring at a tangled length of wire poking out of a bloody bone. He returned some 20 minutes later, reinjected me and eventually dragged the warped bit of metal through the bone. The poor nurse was holding my hand for support and nearly disappeared under the bed with pain herself. I had two similar pins holding the elbow in place, although they were much longer. Fortunately, they were removed much easier, but still under local anaesthetic in the ward.

I was taken once again on the milk float down the dark tunnel and out and over the fields to the theatre. Under general anaesthetic I went again in order for them to separate my leg from the traction bar screwed through my shin bone. This was now March 1978. As I came out from my induced sleep, I was still in the theatre. Only when I was fully awake could the plaster be fitted. As my blurry eyes cleared, I was aware of a crowd gathered around me. It was then I realised I was completely naked, ready for my plaster. As I focused a little better, my eyes looked directly into the eyes of a student nurse, Sharon Atkins. Sharon was in my class at school, and to be honest, I quite fancied her, especially as her dad ran an off licence. 'Hi, Sharon, how are you?' I said groggily.

She looked me up and down like a chef deciding which cut of meat to cook, then said, 'A bit better than you.' In my defence, that operating theatre was freezing cold!!!

The plaster was fitted and I had to spend around two days being turned on the bed, like a rotisserie chicken, in order for the plaster to dry. Three nurses were charged with this duty. During my time in hospital, I had gotten very friendly with some of them, a little too friendly with a couple of them. To the extent I had one nurse, Christine, banging on the metal-framed window one night and shouting, 'I want to see him, but his girlfriend is there every bloody day.'

My girlfriend at the time was now Mandy, the one I had so heroically thrown myself over on the coach to Orient. Nigel and Mandy had split up and she was extremely keen on me after my show of chivalry.

During one of the turns, Christine positioned herself between the Matron and Staff Sister. As the three sets of arms made their way under me, I felt a distinctive grab at the only exposed part of my anatomy. Matron asked as I jolted, 'Is everything okay?'

'Yes, fine, thank you,' I replied. Christine returned later to apologise, whilst wearing the biggest smile.

Before I was allowed to leave hospital, I had to convince the physiotherapist that I could tackle stairs and move around. Unfortunately, as my elbow was so badly damaged and I would never be able to straighten my arm fully again, I was unable to use conventional crutches. So, consequently, I had one ordinary metal one and another that was sort of T-shaped with a strap to wrap around the forearm and secured by Velcro. It was handy if I was in a busy pub, though, because I always had somewhere to lean. In fact, after I started my career in the pub industry, I used to tell some gullible people that my bent arm was the reason I became a licensee... mimicking the action of pulling a pint with the bent elbow at the perfect angle to hold the pump.

The day I got to go home, coincidentally, happened to be Mandy's birthday, and she was having a party at a pub in Fishponds. The plaster I'd had fitted did not permit sitting – it was stand up or lie down. In order to get to the party, Dad brought his van home from work and I was slid into the back and supported with pillows.

My parents also brought my bed down and put it up in the front room. All the old gang came round to see me, and after an enormous amount of celebrating and Rich knocking back the best part of a bottle of Pernod, he was found slumped over the garden wall, talking remarkably sensibly, but unable to actually move. As he only lived in the next street, we debated whether to leave him there and let him walk home when he was able. Eventually, my brother Dave picked him up and carried him home.

Within a week, I had to return to hospital to have the plaster refitted. It had cracked around the top of the leg, courtesy of Mandy. I told you she was keen!!!

Although the plaster was extremely limiting for normal movement, I didn't let it stop me from getting around, managing to walk into town on the crutches and still enjoying the local pub. Playing pool was interesting, though, because every time I bent over to play a shot, my right leg would have to shoot out behind me. More than once, some unfortunate person would trip over the protruding limb.

Eventually, after three months, the doctors thought it safe to remove the Hip Spiker, but only in order to fit me with a supportive leg iron. By wearing this I could remove it to start hydrotherapy. After such a long time, the leg had wasted away and it needed months of physiotherapy. In all, I was off work for eleven months.

Even the doctor gave a comedic performance at my expense when they started to take my cast off. Just as the last piece was removed, he looked over and said, 'Good, I think you should now... have a bath!' I did hum a bit; not surprising really.

My company had kept my job open, even though I had been off 'sick' for so long. I returned to the noise and grime and familiar smell of oil and Swarfega. My right arm was still painfully weak, but because I was always left-handed it was difficult to work on strengthening it. Until I got back to work, that is. Tommy the foreman was still there and he gave me my first job. 'Right, lad, you can work on the fly press.' A mind-numbing job by any stretch of the imagination, but I was pleased to be back. The fly press is what it says, but it's a manually operated one. The job given was to put inserts into holes on the bottom of an aluminium chair base, five for each base. You then swing a large weighted handle to force the inserts home. 'If we see you using your left arm, you'd better duck.'

Sure enough, by habit I'd revert to my left arm and within seconds I'd be bombarded by anything that came to hand. Usually rivets or bolts. I quickly learned my lesson and the help they gave my recovery was invaluable.

It was a good year, following my release from hospital, before I felt confident enough to venture back to my old ways.

BACK IN THE GAME

My physiotherapy was going well and I had regained full strength in my leg, and my arm was back to about 80%. It was never going to fully recover, but I was going to put it to the test.

The rise of the football 'firms' had begun, and clubs up and down the country had varying degrees of notoriety. You didn't have to be in the First Division to have a big determined following; in fact, it sometimes seemed the lower, not-so-successful teams from the more deprived areas had the more notorious crews. The reputation of West Ham's ICF (Inter City Firm), Chelsea had their Head-hunters, Carlisle United's Border City Firm, Stoke City had the Naughty Forty, Luton Town were the MIGS, Leicester City's Baby Squad and The Zulu Warrior's from Birmingham were all to be taken seriously. The list was exhaustive and the names varied. Top of the list, though, were Millwall, and the various groups that followed them, like F Troop and the Treatment. No firm at Bristol Rovers back then, although in recent years The Gas Hit Squad has put their name about. In the early eighties, though, we were just a collection of like-minded twenty-something's standing on the Tote End; we were 'The Tote', and Millwall, the top dogs, funnily enough led by Harry the Dog, were coming to town. We would be ready.

The current affairs programme *Panorama* were making a documentary about this very subject and following the adventures of the South London team. We knew this, and as with all 'big' games the Tote was filling up earlier than usual. The pubs had been foregone in order to protect our sacred shed.

The kick-off was getting close and nothing yet!!! The usual *modus operandi* as an away fan was to know who you are with, split into small groups and arrange to meet at a particular spot on the home fans' end. Sounds easy, it's not. At the smaller grounds we generally travelled to with lower numbers of home participants, you get recognised as not one of them, so you have no choice but to just kick off with what you've got. A good few flurries of punches and see if they bottle it. If not, take a few with you as you try to survive until the Old Bill intervenes and chucks you out. Always a good feeling if you have to exit along the pitch to the applause from your own, usually at the other end of the ground.

'Millwall where are you? Millwall where are you?' we sang, waiting for the inevitable. A young lad came to us and said he thought there were Millwall down there. Three or four of us moved down to where he indicated, a few steps down the terrace.

'Where are these Millwall fuckers, then?' said a lad from work, who, by the way, was just recovering from being run over while pissed and believing he was a sleeping policeman.

Thwack, a long swinging right connected squarely on his jaw from the bloke stood next to him. Then he was off on his toes as we gave chase. Instantly all around him, the Tote descended and he disappeared in a hailstorm of kicks and punches. We returned to sentry duty, waiting for the next event.

'Good work flushing him out,' I said, as my work colleague rose, rubbing his face.

'Your turn next,' he said, laughing.

It became apparent that no large-scale assault would be coming, as every now and again in different areas two or three Londoners would shout out and would immediately be dealt with, the last one being pursued closely by a mob including me, until I was pushed over and received a parting back heel in the mouth from the Deptford boy.

Each attack was repelled, and they left Bristol without enhancing their reputation. We later heard that Harry and the company's bus had broken down on the motorway, so we were spared the pleasure. It was also rumoured that the TV company had coerced the few unfortunate Millwall stalwarts to have a go, as it would make good viewing.

The first time I realised the Tote had some real leaders was at the end of an FA Cup tie with Southampton at Eastville in 1978. First Division Southampton were expecting a win, even on our quagmire of a pitch. They hadn't reckoned with Paul Randall, the latest hero dragged from local non-league football and worked in a supermarket, to set the terraces alight as he scored for fun.

The hordes of Southampton fans massed on the Open End terrace, a huge curved structure that had held 12,000 in earlier years, started to show displeasure as the game drew to a close. They were behind to a magical couple of strikes from our scoring sensation and the inevitable pitch invasion started. They were corralled back onto the dog track as fencing and advertising boards were strewn around. The intention was to get the game abandoned, but the referee soldiered on, and great credit to him for that. However, this wasn't uncommon at the time and the players just carried on regardless, aware, of course, that a warning from the ref before he blew the whistle would assist the players to dive to safety down the tunnel.

The whistle finally went and a huge cheer erupted around the ground, but the Tote were poised for what we hoped was coming. Sure enough, a mass invasion came, and the long-haired and baggy-trousered youth from the South Coast poured onto the pitch, heading for us at the other end. Instantly, we started to mount the wall in a full-on charge.

'Wait, wait!' shouted several 'generals' all along the wall. '**Don't go, wait for them.**'

We waited patiently; our leaders didn't need us running half the length of a muddy pitch, let the prey come to us. On they charged, screaming and roaring with anger at the defeat to the lower division team. Over the halfway line now.

'**Let them come, let them come, get ready!!**'

They were now at our end of the pitch and, unbeknown to them, we were all around the wall of the Tote End, which encircled them on three sides.

'**Go, go, now, now, get the fuckers!**'

The mass ranks poured over the wall. Leaping the hare rail and across the dog track, avoiding the immaculately tended flowerbeds, we attacked. Both corner flags were ripped out and swung mercilessly at the slipping fans, who had stopped their advance as soon as we began ours. Off they ran as fast as they could; some tried to escape to the stands but were repelled by the North Stand mob. Some stood for a while, but soon succumbed to the blue wave that swept over the pitch where only minutes earlier their team had been embarrassed, and now it was their turn.

A glorious sight, watching the hundreds run as they were chased fully out of the ground, across the pitch and up and over the open end and out onto the cinder car park.

Approaching 20 years of age now, and Cardiff at home. A local derby with all the ferocity of a game against the red half of Bristol. Match days at the time during a particularly depressing period for Rovers started off with drinks in the Black Swan or Dirty Duck, as it became known. My brother and I and several friends also used to use it before enjoying the delights of the Dog House Night Club, situated at the Rovers ground and so named because of the greyhound racing track that encircled the pitch. I felt it could have been named for the quality of some of the female customers. Some, not all, I might add.

The Dirty Duck was and still is a wide building on Stapleton Road, next to the once-modern Concorde cinema, and a stone's throw from Eastville Stadium, our home ground. Stapleton Road itself is the main thoroughfare through Easton, dotted with boozers and Indian textile shops, the occasional takeaway where you could eat a different cuisine every night of the week. The railway station was around a quarter of a mile further from the ground. Back then, the whole area had a feeling of despair, a scruffy, run-down inner city, probably not unlike dozens of other towns at the beginning of the '80s.

The pub itself had a bar at the front which ran the length of the building; at the back, entered from a side entrance in the car park, was a smaller bar which, up a step or two, had a couple of pool tables.

At the counter you could see through to the front, as well as entering it from a door opposite to the entrance to this bar.

Our numbers were poor around this time, and at 12.45pm there were no more than 25 to 30 fans in. Having said that, I knew a few of them, and what we lacked in numbers that day we made up for in determination and ability.

The front bar was filling up, and it became apparent very quickly that they were our international visitors from across the Bristol Channel, and they were arriving in numbers. We were all getting a little twitchy on our side of the divide, knowing that this was going to kick off. Cardiff were always up for it and had a reputation that preceded them. Once again it looked like we were outnumbered. I was walking away from the bar with two fresh pints. A few Cardiff 'scouts' came into our bar. A well-known Rovers fan called Maff stood up to meet them. He was a tall, broad, confident man, strong and intelligent, and destined to become a Tote legend. I hurried up to the pool table to safely deposit the drinks, picked up an empty pint glass and returned to the meet. Through the gap you could see the Welsh boys craning to see what was happening. A strange quiet descended as the two parties sized each other up. I was a few paces back as other boys had stepped up to greet the invaders.

The inaction was painful, so I launched the glass at them. It bounced harmlessly off the shoulder of a Cardiff fan, but that was the green light that was required. Eureka, the Rovers Boys took the hint and flew at them. I joined the fray as best I could, wriggling my way to the front line, and the Cardiff gang retreated through both doors and into their bar. We followed them and bundled our way into the front bar. We found ourselves in a confined space, flailing away like lunatics in a sustained onslaught. We stopped around five foot into their bar and stood our ground. The need to retreat hastily to our own lines became apparent as we were then aware of the huge numbers facing us. Instantly, a barrage of glasses were fired through the gap across the bar in both directions, but initially from the back bar and the remaining Tote boys who couldn't join our assault. This prompted us to move back to the sanctuary of the back bar. The sound of smashing glass drowned out the jukebox, but not the screams of the fleeing bar staff. The landlord vainly tried to protect his stock, staff and himself without success, eventually diving for cover and retreating to safety. The Police arrived from all angles, and the crescendo of destruction died down as quickly as it started. The Cardiff fans were escorted out and taken direct to the open end of our cauldron-shaped home. We were then all ejected, so we walked out of the bar and to the car park. Blood spatters were everywhere, up the wall and on the smashed panes of glass and over the floor trailing outside. Fifteen minutes of mayhem: not one bit of blood spilt by us, 150 glasses destroyed and the shelves cleared of cigarettes by the Cardiff fans. It was only just gone 1pm, too early for the football, so my brother and I walked off to the Greenbank pub for a little peace and quiet!!

The 'fun' kept coming; these incidents were frequent and as brutal as they were mainly brief. The Police had sharpened up their game and this in turn, as the eighties progressed, led to the more serious firm meets, sometimes miles from stadiums, and the onset of weapons started to rear its ugly head. I was principally a football fan who would stand my ground if trouble started. Always ready, but the organised encounters were never for me.

In recent years, in order to move with the times and to attempt to achieve the promised land of the Premiership, many clubs have, through rich ownership, managed to construct modern stadiums, all shiny and new; but in doing so, some have lost their soul and that connection to the community. It's like the corner shop going to the out-of-town shopping centre. It's necessary in order to progress, but the atmosphere is never the same. An example could be West Ham moving to the huge round bowl of the Olympic Stadium. The Old Boleyn ground had a great atmosphere and I know is missed by West Ham fans that I know personally.

The old grounds, from our point of view, were at the time preferable to the shiny new stadiums. Firstly, they had been built in the towns, the heartland of their support, and consequently there were more pubs to use; secondly, the stadiums generally had defined ends, easy to identify and infiltrate. An example of this was during another excursion along the M4, this time to Reading and the old Elm Park Stadium. This would have been the late eighties, and I had hired a tatty Transit and filled it with some of our more 'enthusiastic' lads.

After a few drinks on the way into the town, we parked the van a good distance from the ground. A small group of us in one's and two's managed to get onto their end. Our supporters were gathered at the open end and filling up fast. The Reading terrace was down the side of the ground, with the open end to our right as we looked at the pitch. The pitch was the last thing on our minds as we scanned the area for other Gasheads. There had already been a couple of groups in and impatiently they had immediately begun to herald their arrival.

A few swift punches and kicks and panic stations from the home supporters before the Police intervened and ejected the invaders. Our downfall was this very lack of patience. If we could all have bided our time and had a little nod to each other and waited for us all to arrive, the effect there would have been utter pandemonium. However, we didn't have the necessary organisation, and so, like the groups before us, we also raised our voices and hit out at any target. For my part, I leapt onto the shoulders of some tall, overweight lad and began haphazardly hitting around the side of his head as he panicked and tried to race to the exit. He was a big unit and luckily he never fell backwards onto me, where I would certainly have been trapped and crushed. I dismounted and raced back to the fray. In hindsight, it was rather comical really.

Once again the Police were in, trying to encircle the aggressors. They managed to eject most of us pitch-side and we sauntered off towards the applauding crowd assembled at the open end. From our vantage point we could still see some of the guys from our van. There were still around four or five of them, separated but aware of each other. The players filed out onto the pitch and shortly before the start of the game, and with more of us standing in their end, off it went again. A huge cheer and charge from the open end as we watched the Berkshire fans scatter. Throughout the game there was a feeling of animosity. The Reading fans had become a little braver now that they thought all of our boys had been removed. Way into the game, and suddenly they panicked again. There, stood in the middle of an ever-increasing circle, was Rod. More on this man later, where his legendary status will be revealed.

Not one of them were interested in the slightest of going anywhere near him, and he was also able to do the march of honour.

At the end of the game we were locked in behind some tall metal corrugated gates. The crowds were filing out and a crush began. Women and children were beginning to panic, and then there was a huge push and the gates fell like a drawbridge, slamming onto the road outside and startling the Reading fans walking past. The masses of Bristol youth poured out onto the dark streets of Reading and once again the young Royals fans fled for all they were worth from the riotous mob. Immediately the chase began. We were running up the road in pursuit and watching bodies disappear over hedges and trying to duck away down side alleys. The stragglers escaped as the pursuit chased a group over the large park. My days of blindly chasing after people who were intent on running away as fast as they could had already passed me by, and I only followed as it was conveniently on the way to the van.

Don't think for a minute that every game home or away was mindless acts of hooliganism; nothing could be further from the truth. We would travel far and wide, often grabbing a drink or two in the local pubs and talking with locals. If we were welcomed.

Unfortunately, there have been times when the fun has been ruined, and usually by the Police.

On one of several visits to Fulham, a large crowd of both Bristol and Fulham fans were in a pub – long gone now – called the Kings Arms, on the bend of the new Kings Road. One suitably dressed Rovers fan – eye patch, fake cutlass, the lot – was leading the room in a masterly rendition of *Delilah*. The Old Bill descended on us and ordered the pub to be shut. Some raw Hendon snot decided to snatch Colin's cider. Well, that was like taking a bone from a Rottweiler: Colin kept a firm grasp and a battle of wills ensued.

'Put it down!'

'I will when I've drunk it, mate.'

'Put it down. Let go.'

'I'm still drinking it. I've paid for it and I'm going to drink it.'

'I'm telling you to put it down.'

'I'm telling you I will, when it's empty.'

The Police started shoving people out into the road, where half the Met were out with all the toys; horses, dogs and the meat wagons. I DIDN'T THINK THE SINGING WAS THAT BAD.

Colin eventually broke off his chat with Officer Dribble, and as he was walking out another of our brave Bobbies gave him a good whack across the legs. Colin turned and reacted – just what they wanted. One more for the van.

Another trip to Tranmere was more notable for the journey home than the day out. A full coach with several pick-up points around North Bristol, and we were off. We arrived in Birkenhead in good time and made our way to a suitable pub. As we walked in, some of the older locals in broad scouse accents welcomed us. A few drinks, the game and a planned stop in Chester on the way home. The coach driver was known by some of the lads: an affable Irishman who just sat at the bar while we enjoyed the hospitality of the Bristolian landlord in Chester's historic town centre.

We only noticed that the driver had secretly indulged in a few pints along with the rest of us during the drive home, which was terrifying, to say the least, but the desire to get home at any cost trumped the fact we might die in some horrific fireball. A lot of drink will do that. Careering down the motorway, we all became aware that lorries were almost trying to hem us in, horns blaring. We pulled into a services and the coach was driven straight over a huge kerb. God alone knows how we made it back in one piece.

Stranger still, the passenger list read like a who's who of Tote boys, as the bus started depositing its cargo of Bristol's finest, starting in Kingswood, Fishponds, and then a couple of us, me included, at the corner of Eastville Park, before going on to Lockleaze, Filton and Patchway.

We staggered off the coach around 2.30am and started the walk down towards Easton. The window of a car parked where we had got off opened and a voice in the dark whispered, 'Good game today, lads'; then off it sped after the meandering coach. I can only assume the local Constabulary were wisely waiting for the numbers to decrease sufficiently before making their move.

Home games could be lively, depending on the opponents. 1980, and Rovers are riding high, division-wise, for our under-achieving team. Today it would be the Championship or the Second Division, before the Premiership came into being. Our opponents were Chelsea and we knew there would be trouble as again the Chelsea Head Hunters were forging a reputation. The Gasheads' meeting place around this time was the Queens Head at the top of Royate Hill, across the green expanse of Eastville Park. The pub was a large, ornate, red-brick building, with a long serving bar running fully 10 yards and then bending at the end to follow the building. Boasting a lounge bar and high ceilings, it had the appearance of a traditional London pub. At the back it had a large beer garden and a hardstanding at the front for no more than eight cars. This was a local pub serving the tight little streets set behind the building and the surrounding Fishponds area. Some 200 of us had congregated and were milling around, scanning the busy Fishponds Road that separated the pub from the park. Some were walking around already armed with clubs and pool cues, expecting the massed ranks of Chelsea to appear over the horizon at any time. A couple of unfortunate away fans arrived and, because they showed no humility, were swiftly dealt with by a small group outside. One of them escaped after a few swift kicks, running for his life, but another one was battered unconscious and was left flat out on the hardstanding outside the pub. An ambulance was called and the ridiculous sight of his attackers helping him onto the vehicle was ironic.

There were no further arrivals to this safe house, and the time came for us to leave. Everybody poured out and across the road, forcing all traffic to stop. Now nearer 300 strong, we all climbed the grass bank and the wave swept across the open playing fields. In doing so, several park football matches that were in progress had to also stop in their tracks, as this huge mob rampaged across the pitches, stealing the balls away and scoring the odd beauty in the process. Local dog walkers immediately changed the route they were following and briskly moved in opposite directions. The horde of alcohol-fuelled hooligans ran on down towards the end of the park, where the M32 loomed large above us. The Police were there to meet this army and tried to guide us left and down the side of the motorway towards the home end and, of course, the Tote End. Our plans that day were different, as we all to a man pressed on swarming through and brushing the hapless lawmen out of the way as we leapt the railings and ran under the subways and across the busy lanes of traffic on the motorway junction's roundabout. The intention was to enter the ground from the Muller Road entrance across the cinder car park, where the Chelsea fans would be entering. The Police were swept aside, powerless to resist this unstoppable force. Running across the cinders, swerving around the cars, we could see in the distance in the corner a large group of away supporters queuing to file through the battered turnstile cubicles.

A huge roar rose as we charged towards them from 100 yards or so, while the Chelsea fans turned and spotted us and an almighty scramble to get in ensued. As we closed, they had no choice but to turn and stand, and a good old-fashioned scrap got going as everyone there started swinging with pure animosity. I was dressed in familiar attire for the day, with a brand new sheepskin coat and the obligatory Doc Martens. Others on both sides of this battle were wearing matching uniforms to shield from the winter's cold. We flew at them and I managed to land a good blow onto one of the enemy, so that his head jolted back and cracked against the concrete blockwork wall. As he started to slide down the wall, stunned, I decided I might try and relieve him of his coat and attempted to wrestle it off him. God knows why, and thankfully my attempt failed. Again, the Police arrived quickly to stop the assault, which was as vicious as it was swift. As we retreated and headed away towards the Tote End, I looked down and noticed I had a new buttonhole on the front of my coat: a perfect inch-long slash from a Stanley knife. I wished I had got his coat after seeing the damage. In hindsight, though, these coats were great protection, as the use of Stanley knife blades and other weapons were starting to become commonplace.

Every few paces on the walk around the ground there were scuffles and stand-offs. Chelsea were here in force, riding high in the table, and were going to give a better showing than Millwall did for *Panorama*.

We had made an error staying in the pub too long, and Chelsea had managed to get good numbers onto the Tote, causing panic on a sparsely occupied terrace. The Police were already in with dogs and a horse or two, trying to keep the two sides separated. Chelsea, though, had taken the centre ground under the main shed behind the goal. As we all filed through the turnstiles, the desire to rush up and put this liberty right was all-consuming, but we had to wait for the majority to click, click, click through the gates. We all assembled outside and split into a two-pronged attack. The group I was with ascended the high steps at the back and the others went around to the right. As we arrived from the sunlight into the dark, we could see the young 'uns' relief as we poured down towards the invaders. The Police lines stayed strong. We charged again with the rest farther down the terrace. The Police line started to move back, shepherding the Londoners away and around the curved structure. The noise was deep and intimidating; no joyful songs, just chants of hatred and venom. All sorts of missiles were being thrown from both sides, including coins and bottles and anything else that came to hand. I was sure a shoe went sailing past at one stage.

The Police continued moving the Chelsea fans away, aware that we were now almost at full force. Chelsea had made the young Tote End boys run, but the Tote were there now and we were doing our utmost to get at them. Eventually, as was usual, the Police managed to get them all onto the dog track and they all sauntered off towards the open end, to the adulation of the thousands of their fans gathered there. As they were going over the fence, a couple of good charges went in, and several of us got close enough to land a few farewell whacks.

We won the game 3-0 and the usual disorder at the other end went off, but again it was an unsuccessful attempt to abandon the game.

Outside in the car park after the game and in the dark, a good few of us were standing waiting, at the orders of a giant of a man, to stand and fight. The large crowd were filtering past us, and this Goliath was peering through the crowd, looking for a likely victim. The majority of the Chelsea fans had exited via Muller Road, but we knew some of their more 'enthusiastic' support might return this way. True enough, and without warning, the bloke – who must have stood 6ft 5in or even bigger – threw a big thick heavy arm full into an unsuspecting enemy. Before the unconscious one had hit the deck, he singled out another victim and delivered a similar punishment. We all stood ready and found our own targets, leading to a short brawl before the familiar intervention from the Hi-Viz gang with their ultimate deterrent: the barking, snarling, biting dogs.

INDEPENDENCE AND HOW TO USE IT

Aged 21, and my first car. It had taken a while to pass my test due to my hospitalisation. Mum and Dad had a friend who was selling his Mark II Cortina 1600 automatic. Column change, in flaky silver fox blue. They bought it for me for my birthday for the princely sum of £100.

Within weeks I had set about spending every penny I had on it. Respray to Sierra Beige, bronze vinyl roof, hair-raiser spotlights – I'd even made a centre consul in work, made from mild steel. I was by now a welder, so why wouldn't I? I covered it in a bit of vinyl – loved the smell of that glue – and all the switches and cassette deck slotted in to it. I don't think all the modifications helped the performance much, which was woeful, but I loved that car. Even in 1981 the paint job cost £500, so you can see the commitment I made.

Independence! Swindon away, we can take my car. Drive up, no mucking about, and back home to make the pub for a couple.

Before the game we had taken over the closest pub to the ground, the County Ground Hotel, and everyone was in very high spirits, with all sorts of dodgy drinking games and the usual stories being told. No sign of any Swindon fans, and with the mob that had congregated, probably just as well.

The first bit (watch the game) went well; then things took a turn.

Five of us in the car, including Colin, his older brother Martin, my old mate Rich and me. I can't for the life of me remember who else was with us.

Driving out around a large open area, to our right a large group of Swindon fans started chucking rocks in our direction. **'Wankers! I've just had this painted.'**

I rammed the column change gear lever to park and the car slewed to a screeching halt. In an instant we all piled out of the car; three of us – Rich, Martin and Colin – had located weapons of sorts in the car, but I bent and grabbed a rock to return fire. A Transit van came racing up and braked in a similar fashion. The back doors burst open and out poured more Bristol boys straight into the attack. The Wiltshire mob turned tail immediately just as the Police arrived to save us a fruitless chase.

'Did you see what those pricks were throwing at my car?'

'All right, all right, get back in and fuck off, the lot of you,' snorted plod.

'Cheers, lads!' I shouted towards the Transit. They gave a thumbs-up from the van and off they went, singing at the tops of their voices.

Further down the road, but still not out of Swindon, we stopped at a chip shop, parking the car down a back alley. We got our food and were just standing facing the busy road. There were two lanes of traffic coming from our right and a double-decker bus approached in the far lane. It seemed to be packed with people leaving the football, and as I looked upstairs towards the front of the bus, I saw some fat prick giving us the wanker sign.

If you recall, I blamed my fractured skull as a child on a lot of my behaviour, and now seems like an apt time to tell you of the type of ways it manifests itself.

When this, for want of a better word, fog hits me, I seem to have tunnel vision. I'm aware of things around me, but have no control over my actions, however brief they may be. Luckily, as I have got older these episodes have become rarer, so much so that I can't remember the last time I experienced one. I still suffer excruciating headaches which, when they start, I know I will be burdened with for several days. The first time I remember this happening, I was probably eleven or twelve at senior school. In a classroom and from behind, a friend of mine as a joke cracked me not too hard over the head with a thick red maths text book. In a buzzing tunnel-view flash, I reacted, and Jerry was on the floor with a desk on top of him. I had no recollection of doing it; suffice to say he never played a trick like that again. I still dislike being tapped or rubbed on my head.

Anyway, I handed Rich my food parcel and ran across the traffic to the bus. The tunnel vision located the emergency door open lever and I pulled it. I jumped onto the bus and was aware of the driver looking over his shoulder towards me. Scanning the area, I started to climb the stairs. I heard a scream from somewhere, but pressed on. As I reached the upper level, I was facing the back of the bus. All the time I could hear a loud humming noise. My tunnel view rotated to the right to locate our fat friend. He looked like he was about to shit himself as I leant over and repeatedly punched him and watched his flabby mug bounce off the window. No one moved a muscle to help him. In fact, I was sure the kid sat next to him got his football programme out and buried his face in it, hoping he wasn't next.

Unchallenged, I walked back down the stairs, off the bus and across the road to retrieve my meal.

'You're fucking mental,' said Rich.

'**You can talk, you bleeding stabbed me when we were kids. Anyway, I only hit him a couple of times.**'

'His head hit that window at least twenty times,' he said.

The following year, early in the season we had played Swindon again, winning 5-0 or 5-1, and the van we were in stopped in Chippenham. As we were drinking in the high street, a local lad started talking to Colin and me. 'It's fucking great having Rovers here tonight; they're all fucking Swindon or City here... Hey, did you hear about that Rovers kiddie who got on a bus last year and belted some Swindon fan?'

Colin piped up, 'Yes, do you want his autograph?', nodding in my direction.

Later, somehow, the lid of a postbox outside the pub was removed, all the letters grabbed and the pillar box filled with empty glasses. The lid was sent spinning down the high street. Once back in the van, it didn't take long before the familiar sight of flashing blue lights was around us and we found ourselves back to the nick for several hours of interrogation.

We were all turfed out of the van and paraded in front of the Desk Sergeant. He informed us of the seriousness of tampering with the royal mail, blah, blah. 'You are all in the shit now...,' he continued.

Then another of us was found in the back of the van under a load of coats. He'd been in there a while and was absolutely shitfaced, and the first thing he had to say was, 'You can't hang a man with a wooden leg!' Everyone looked at him bemused, before he added the line, 'You've got to use rope.'

The Desk Sergeant's mood darkened even more, because some other bright spark was asking the rest of the group, 'Which one of you lot is Postman Pat?'

I honestly only knew a few of the guys in the van; they were all from the Lockleaze area, a staunch, solid Rovers estate. Some real characters as well. Earlier that evening, while rallying around the country lanes of Wiltshire looking for a decent pub, one of the boys climbed out of the front window onto the roof and slid the length of the van, to be hauled back in through the back doors. We found a pub and the landlord was doing a barbeque in the garden. His shoulders physically slumped as we arrived. We all poured out in very high spirits and within a few minutes one of the Lockleaze boys was on the flat roof with the pub's 'A' board, declaring the end of the world was nigh. The landlord was cooking and brandishing a very large chef's knife, politely asking us to leave. There were families at this soiree, and after a quiet pint we left without any further disturbance.

In the interview room with some or other detective, he said, 'Do you know how serious this is? Tampering with the Royal Mail.'

'I do now.'

'If we take fingerprints, are we going to find yours on these letters?'

'Probably.'

'What?'

'Well, they were being chucked about all over the place in there; when they landed on me, I just picked them up and put them in the middle.'

'Who broke the mail box?'

'No idea. To be honest, I don't really know any of them. I got let down on my original lift and just jumped in with these guys,' I tell Inspector Clouseau.

Shortly after 4am, we were let out. A couple of us were charged, but I doubted any of it would stick.

Another opportunity to get up country for a game came around. My wife at the time hailed from the Midlands and had two sisters, one younger and the other the eldest, who lived in Sheffield. We would all share the duty of visiting each other when we could. The youngest lived up on the Wirral near Liverpool, so always a good weekend to be had. Our turn to go to Yorkshire had come around, and as luck would have it, Rovers were due to play Sheffield United.

I convinced my wife that Colin should come with us and we could go to the match while she spent the time catching up with the two girls. Her sister lived in a large detached house on the south side of Sheffield, and a bed was made up for Colin on the floor of the box room. The girls dropped us off outside Bramall Lane at 11, and we arranged for a pick-up around 6.30pm, to allow time for a couple of après football drinks. At the side of the ground was a small pub called The Sportsman, and the pub sign depicted a Sheffield United player. I said to Colin maybe later, but let's get away from the ground and find somewhere for a quiet drink.

Well, we walked about a mile north and found a large boozer sheltered by tall blocks of flats. An estate pub, but we were thirsty as always. We walked in and the place already had around twenty red and white-clad Blades fans in. If someone had been playing a piano, he would have stopped as the whole room stopped and looked at these strangers entering the 'saloon'.

'Got any cider, love?' barked Colin in his broad Bristolian accent.

'Fuck!' I thought, but chuckled to myself at the same time. A couple of them rose from their seats. Even the jukebox seemed to have stopped mid-song, waiting to see what happened next.

I caught the eye of one of them and offered an 'all right?' nod. Luckily, the troops stood down as the barmaid blew the dust off a Blackthorn font and served a couple of rank but cold pints. We had a few and a good-natured chat with the local lads, and eventually found ourselves in the Sportsman pub with our new buddies. Pissed as farts, we stumbled into the ground and had no recollection of the game at all, other than we lost 3-2. We managed another couple after the game in a pub across a spot of wasteland and awaited our lift. All in all, a good afternoon.

The following morning, as we prepared to drive home, the girls couldn't get over how tidy Colin had left his room, even making his bedding up into a bed pack. That's prison life for you.

HISTORY

The two professional football clubs in Bristol, certainly as far back as I can remember, have always had a fierce rivalry. The early '70s right through the 1980s and the '90s. The reasons are many. Some are geographical – as a general rule of thumb, go south of the river to Bedminster, Southville, Knowle and Ashton, to mention a few, and it's likely the inhabitants are City fans. Or Shitheads as we like to call them. More on the reason in a while. For Rovers or Gasheads, the north is more home turf: Patchway, Kingswood, Eastville, Lockleaze and Filton, again to name a few. It's also the crossroads of two counties: Somerset and Gloucestershire. Bristol does hold its own county status, but purely for administration reasons, I feel. Family ties could affect your allegiance, or even your own personal preference. To change allegiance is rare, but not unheard of.

The history of these nicknames derives from around the early '70s and has been well documented.

Basically, as Eastville Stadium stood next to an old Gas Works, there were times when a smelly cloud of effluent would waft across the site. This prompted the City fans into a nose-grabbing exercise, along with a rather childish chant of 'Smelly, gaasss, gaasss', with the moniker Gasheads soon being given.

Back then, a sub-group of the Tote, a burly greaser mob called the Tramps, after an embarrassing defeat to City at home, followed the schoolgirl City fans chanting to St Pauls and attacked. The chanting ceased and the running ensued. Fleeing for all they were worth.

As quickly as we received this name, which now supersedes our actual nickname of The Pirates, the 'Gas' fans quickly appointed one for them. Now what rhymes with City? Of course, Shitty. Perfect.

So they quickly became Shitheads. Here ends the lesson.

In the context of my story so far, I have referred to us as Rovers, because then that's who we were. Today, everyone – be it fan, or manager or TV pundit – just always calls us The Gas. We lap it up; better than being The Shit, surely?

GROWING UP, BUT NOT AS YOU KNOW IT

The event on the bus at Swindon had given me a little kudos, and some of the older, harder, hardcore members of the Tote started to recognise me. Don't get me wrong, it was still me. I wasn't suddenly some big-name lunatic. It was a nod of 'all right', and I'm sure some of them don't know my name to this day. I was probably one of many who, in our own little way, were trying to promote and preserve the growing reputation of the Tote End. But I was now standing in the same spot as my early day heroes. At the back to the left, up under the smaller shed. Entrance from the steps to our left and entrance from the side below us. We were the Guards; from there, any invaders who would try to attack the noisy rank and file 'young 'uns' section under the huge shed directly behind the goal, would get a shock, as we would dive in from above or behind. I did get friendlier with an absolute Tote Legend, who sadly passed away some years ago. Rod was a good six foot-plus tall, with laser blue eyes. Very intelligent, with an encyclopaedic knowledge of capital cities. Rod, of course, was mentioned earlier during our trip to Reading.

I'm not sure when we got to know each other, but obviously it was at the football. He lived on the 15th floor of a block of flats in Easton, about half a mile from where I lived at the other end of Easton Road. Originally from the Lockleaze area, he was an absolute clean freak and hated any sort of dirt. He once owned a Ford Corsair which had some fuel issues, and although not a mechanic, I did have a basic knowledge and said I'd have a look. He flatly refused to let me hold his Haynes manual for fear I get a spot of oil on it, and I had to crane my neck to look at the pictures and instructions. Another time, he had returned from holiday and we were in his flat. The fridge had some eggs in it left over from before he went away. 'They've gotta go,' he said. So we took half a dozen eggs and threw them from the balcony, trying to make it competitive and hit a few ant-sized pedestrians in the process.

We would trundle around Bristol loaded to the gunnels with sometimes six other lads in my old Maxi 1850, always starting at The Essex Arms in Kingswood, before visiting The Cabot (Royal Oak) on Gloucester Road, then taking in the delights of the Cotham Porter Stores or Highbury Vaults. All pubs that sold his preferred Rough Cider – Scrumpy, to those not from Bristol. There was a night, though, that our pub itinerary was going to change. After Rod called on me, we started on our normal round of hostelries. By the time we had reached Gloucester Road, we had a car full. Next stop was town. The sister of Riff, another Tote lad, had been slapped hard by a Shithead who they knew drank in a pub known as Harry's Bar. 'Harry's' real name was The Bunch of Grapes, situated at the top of a flight of wide stone steps that led down to Baldwin Street, a broad, busy city centre road. The pub itself, on St Nicholas Street, is opposite the covered market with the same name. The pub was a favourite haunt for City fans, and so we were going as a back-up for the avenging brother.

Rod said to park at the bottom of the steps, and we then climbed them to the door of the pub. It was a fine, pleasantly warm evening, and as we got to the top, several of the enemy were milling around outside. Some of them were the main boys and they instantly recognised Rod, immediately looking twitchy, scanning the area and looking down the steps. I walked into the pub and found our man, saying that there were a few of us outside. Rod was talking to the City crew as the rest of our car's passengers stood a pace or two away.

'There he is,' said Stan, the guy standing with Riff, as a tall man walked towards the stairs that went down to the toilets located in the basement.

As Riff followed the target, I returned outside. Within a minute or two, we heard a real commotion, and looking back into the pub we saw the target staggering around, holding his blood-covered face.

'Go and get the car started,' Rod said.

'What about Riff?'

'He's gone out the front door. Get the car started, I'll keep this lot busy.'

Two of us scuttled down the stairs before we were all rumbled. I got into the car and turned the ignition... Nothing. Then on the second turn the engine just turned without starting. I was still trying to start it when the rest of our support group arrived and piled into the car. At last it caught, and we roared off as best you possibly can in an old Maxi. Within 100 yards there was a junction, with Bristol Bridge to the right. But we were turning left, across the end of St Nicholas Street. By this time the mob of Shitheads had twigged what was going on and were racing to intercept us. Luckily, we passed the road in time to receive no more than a hail of glasses. Nice interlude to the evening, we all agreed. At the time, Rovers rarely played City as we were usually in different divisions, although confrontations could happen at any time on any night of the week.

There was a period which was started by City fans when, on another quiet Tuesday night, a car-load of Shitheads called in to the Sugar Loaf pub on St Marks Road in Easton, and, spotting a young Rovers lad in there with his girlfriend, set about them, breaking her jaw in the process, as well as wrecking the bar area. This started a series of tit-for-tat reprisals, culminating in the Colliers, a pub used by City fans, being destroyed by a rampaging mob of 50 or so Gasheads. The damage and injuries were severe enough to make the national press.

***

There was an unwritten law during our pub crawls around north Bristol: the driver never paid for drinks. Back then, drinking and driving was a stupid thing that occurred, and I will hold my hands up and confess I was guilty of it. One Tuesday night almost put paid to it. We had been doing our regular trawl around, starting in Kingswood, then a couple of Gloucester Road pubs, followed by a visit to Cotham and St Michaels Hill. The car had the usual suspects on board: seven or eight predominantly skinhead types. Our penultimate pub prior to finishing the night was the Inkerman in St Pauls.

This was the mid-eighties, and only a few years earlier the area had been rocked by the first in a series of riots across the country. The Inkerman was in the centre of the St Pauls community and was not a place for the faint-hearted. For our part, we had no thoughts of racial differences and I never encountered or considered any prejudices growing up. However, when we left the pub a couple of the guys weren't coming with us to our last stop, The Queens Head on Easton Road, so I stopped to let them out as we left St Pauls and entered Easton on the inner ring road. The Police pulled up behind me. I told my passengers to keep quiet and I jumped out to talk to the officers.

Thinking a breathalyser was coming, I was thankful that I had just had a soft drink in the last pub.

'What you been doing down the Jungle?' asked the lawman.

'I'm sorry, where?' I asked, a little shocked.

'We saw you all leaving the pub, and we've had some trouble with young blokes going down there upsetting the natives.'

'Well, we just called in on the way through. I know a few guys in there. I play pool in there a bit. They've had a drink and I just had a Coke,' I made a point of saying during my nervous ramble.

I was quite shocked at the flippant way this Policeman was talking, but relieved that he seemed to have no interest in my alcohol content. He was, rightly, I guess, trying to preserve the peace in the area, but the language he used would be deemed extremely racist, not only today, but back then too.

He waved us off and we got to our last watering hole for around 10.45pm. This was the latest respectably you should arrive at a pub back then. Especially as all of the local pubs at the time did 'lock ins' and we would expect to be in there until around 1am. It was a Tuesday, after all, and I still had to get to work in the morning, so I wasn't staying out too late!!!

One memory of Rod, and there were many. Leaving the City Ground one night, a big crowd, both sets of fans up for it. The Police escorting The Gas along the road by the side of Ashton Park. We had charged across the Park at the swarming masses of Shithead youth, but were returned to the preferred route by mounted Police and the accompanying officers with dogs. Overhead, a helicopter's blades were whoop, whoop, whooping, and the two sets of fans were in great voice, taunting each other. As we moved along the road with the park to our left, a three-foot wall was the divider and the grass of the park started at that level above us. There was just the street light and torches of the Police escort, horses bucking and chomping on the bridles as they went. Several rabid dogs snarled and barked with foaming mouths, and a deafening combined roar broke out as some 30 or more City fans charged out from the side streets on the other side of us. This was their turf, after all, and a gap opened up as a moment of panic hit the Rovers parade. Instantly, from atop the wall this tall, distinctive figure launched himself into the clearing. As he threw a concussive punch at the nearest invader, above all the cacophony of sound I distinctly heard the City fans shout, 'It's D*******.'

We charged forward with this superhero at the front. We couldn't fail, and the Shitheads disappeared back down the rabbit hole they had ambushed us from.

He said to me one night in a quiet moment, 'It took me 18 months to get my reputation; it will take me the rest of my life to live it down.' His reputation is still alive and will always be. R.I.P.

Around this time I separated from my children's mother. It had been a difficult relationship, started as a 19-year-old and, plied with tumblers of Bacardi by her, I fell into the relationship. Before long she fell pregnant with my daughter, and around two years later my son was born. I tried to support them as best I could on my meagre wage. There were so many problems with the relationship I don't know where to start, and as I expect this to be read by my children, I am not prepared to try.

I left and divided my time living at my brother's house in Eastville and in my uncle's pub in St Pauls. I paid my way at the pub by doing some shifts behind the bar and walking Max the Doberman at night around the subways and lanes bordering the M32 motorway. By this time, due to the shortage of money, I initially kept riding a pushbike to and from work in Fishponds. Leaving work, I was able to use the cycle track and pop in to see the kids most evenings for an hour. The time was precious for me and I did my upmost not to miss the visits.

I would usually get to my uncle's pub, the White Horse on Ashley Down Road, around 6.30pm, just as the pub was opening for the evening. My auntie would prepare a meal for me and it would be kept warm in the oven. One night, as I was removing my plate, I heard a shout from the bar. A troubled soul called Lawrence, who had a fascination with my aunt, had come into the bar, reached over, grabbed a glass and attempted to pour himself a lager. My uncle, normally a gentle, friendly individual, spotted him and told him to stop in no uncertain terms. That is when Lawrence rushed at him and thrust the glass into his stomach, fortunately just scratching him and not doing any more damage. We all joked later that his wallet had deflected the blow. My uncle wrestled Lawrence to the floor, and this is when I heard the shout. Rushing out into the bar, I spotted them both wrestling on the floor and my uncle struggling to restrain him. Without a thought, I struck Lawrence several times in the stomach, and this stopped his writhing temporarily. His stomach was solid, like punching wood, and his demeanour indicated that he had taken some sort of drug. I stood up, we called the Police, and my aunt fetched the dog to further encourage Lawrence to temper his behaviour. I had stood up as he seemed to be a little calmer, when he started to kick and struggle again. My uncle was losing his grip, so I delivered a swift kick to the ribs. This had the desired effect and Lawrence groaned and became much more compliant. An ambulance was also dispatched and he was taken firstly to hospital and then sectioned in a local mental health facility.

Some weeks later, after he had been released, he returned to his flat, which was located in the side street next to the pub. It was where we had to park our cars, and one morning as I left I bumped into him. He jumped back, saying that I had broken three of his ribs. I didn't apologise, just saying that he was out of order and needed controlling. On the back of my car he had scrawled the word 'Thug'. We didn't see him in the pub again.

I got further involved and accepted on the Tote after another away trip, this time just across the bridge to Newport County. All sorts of capers were going on. Another one of our main lads was Charlie. With a crumpled nose and thickset shoulders, he looked a handful, and so he proved on many occasions. Fast hands, he would hit you five times before you blinked; usually, blinking after his opening burst was not possible. As the best part of 40 of us were languishing in the Gwent Police headquarters, aptly named Pentonville, we were all able to detail the various events of the afternoon.

For my part, I had simply entered their end, along with Colin and a couple of other lads. We started singing our little English hearts out to attract the necessary attention, which it did. The paltry crowd that had gathered were egging each other on and I was encouraging the lad at the front to follow his mate's advice. 'Hit him, Dai' – or whatever his name was.

'Yes, come on, Dai, hit me.'

He was shuffling about, trying to pluck up the courage to hit this manic Bristolian stood in front of him.

'Bristol, Bristol, Bristol!' my few mates chimed in. Nothing came from our nervous Welsh boys, then Plod arrived.

'Where you from?' he said to me.

'Down the road, why?'

'Think you'd better leave, don't you?'

'I suppose so,' I said, thoroughly dejected.

I started to walk down the terrace towards the exit. The rest of the Rovers were the other side, across a sort of no-man's land area. I could see Colin just getting to the gate as I heard a noise right behind me. Dai had four more of his sheep-shagging mates standing with him, suddenly looking a little braver.

Good!! At last.

No hesitation, I leapt forward and hit the closest shepherd full in the face. He fell back, holding his mug, and instantly the brave soldiers backed off. Pathetic. I turned away with a shrug and almost immediately I was enveloped by three coppers. Charged with Section 5, threatening behaviour, and a couple of weeks later in court, a £300 fine for my trouble. This was a lot of cash in 1983 and everyone suffered a similar punishment. The Policeman's ball that year must have been something else.

Charlie's little bit of fun had involved chasing some lad down the street and netting him with a dustbin; what a sight that must have been. Him running for all he was worth, then suddenly all the lights going out and he's rolling down a hill in some sort of slapstick sketch.

Pentonville's design was very interesting. Down in the depths of the building, the long corridor consisted of several bar-fronted lock-ups, not unlike the jails in a western movie. I think they were designed to hold eight each, but they were very popular this day and there were at least 12 in our pen. We were in the last cage before the end. At the very end was another one, but the barred door was more the size of a normal cell door. Charlie and several more were deposited in that one. The vast majority of prisoners were Gas, but Charlie's cell contained one unfortunate young lad from Newport.

After a few hours, our hosts brought some food for us, as is required by law, I guess.

'What you got, Charlie?'

'Fucking cheese roll.'

'We've all got ham and cheese in ours.'

'If you give me some ham ones, you can have this little Newport fucker.'

'We don't want him.'

'He's no fucking use to me.'

The poor lad must have been quaking in his socks. Mainly because the corridor was lined with our boots.

Other trips away, and often just a select group would travel in an ordinary Transit van. I hired one myself a few times and had the elite group travelling sometimes 15 to 20 in the back, if you got a long wheelbase. The beauty of the vans was they were unmarked and we took to entering the towns from completely the opposite way, thereby avoiding the attention of the Police, who would be waiting along the presumed routes. As we were driving in, I'd shout, 'Keep your heads down', when in reality it was impossible as so many were crammed in. We were a dedicated bunch, as rarely was there any sort of cushion to sit on, but always plenty to drink.

One trip away and we are meeting in the Punch Bowl on Old Market prior to a long drive to Stoke to play their local neighbours, Port Vale. Nine am and a couple of pints of cider with my full English is enough to set me up. But not for all, as for the first time I saw a few partaking of some illicit substances with the intention, as someone said, 'We can fight all day long on this stuff.' It was never for me; blimey, I never even got tobacco. On this trip a couple of Rovers boys had wandered into the main Port Vale supporters' pub. If my memory serves me right, it was called The Bowler Hat. During the inevitable fracas, one of our lads took a beating and was rendered temporarily blind for a while.

POWER TO THE PEOPLE

I had been getting on well at work. We continued to take the piss, especially on Fridays, when at 12 on the dot we'd all escape to the local pub in Fishponds, usually the Peckett's Flyer, but our allegiance changed frequently. The Spotted Cow or The Greyhound on the Lodge Causeway tempted us from time to time, as did the Full Moon. The Peckett's was closest to work, not that it mattered on a Friday as we rarely went back on time, getting someone with a conscience to clock us in.

I had also started taking an interest in the Union and became shop steward in the A.U.E.W. for a while. The Amalgamated Union of Engineering Workers were a militant group with headquarters on Victoria Street in the centre of town.

The factory we worked in had never really had any cause for disputes, but that was about to change. I don't know how I fell into this role, but I was always able to speak my mind and articulate our demands well.

One year, our annual pay demands were levied with management and the negotiations began to take place. Always a protracted procedure, undertaken by convenors farther up the food chain than I.

Nothing was happening, so a vote to work to rule was passed. I had the honour of informing our Manager, Allan Martins, who was a thin, gangly man with dark hair and a smart dark suit. He always looked troubled, and I often thought he had the appearance of an undertaker. He may have been happier in that profession – no wage negotiations there.

Shortly after the work to rule was imposed, it was felt that one of our members had been victimised. The dander was up and I offered a rallying speech. Before you knew it, we were out the door and on strike, for the first time in the history of the company.

Picket lines were arranged, two gates needed to be guarded, and I cleverly opted for the night duty opposite the Greyhound pub on the Lodge Causeway. Easy: park the car across the entrance and wait for the landlord of the pub to provide warming brews and snacks.

Almost three weeks we stayed on strike. An offer to settle was put to the members on a Thursday afternoon in the car park in front of the local TV news network and under a blazing sun. Of course, all of our demands weren't met, but it came as close as we thought possible, so the chubby middle-aged union convenor, in his baggy, shiny suit, recommended acceptance. The workers unanimously accepted, and with great relief said, 'Shall we go back tomorrow?'

'Hold on, hold on,' I said. 'I know it's been tough, and a struggle for us all, but let's not show the men upstairs our resolve is weak. Sure we will accept the offer, but as an act of defiance and to prove we will not be treated in this way again, I say we return to work on Monday with our heads held high.' My Churchillian speech struck a chord and they all agreed.

Thank God, I thought; Ken, Andy and I can still cycle to Bath on the piss tomorrow like we planned.

The bike ride to Bath was an enjoyable day out and I tried to justify the fact that I had deliberately kept the whole factory out for another day when they had lost enough money during our dispute as just reward for my efforts during the negotiating process.

The old disused railway, my childhood escape route, had been covered to create a cycle path and ran from Lawrence Hill station through Easton, Whitehall, Fishponds and on out of Bristol to Bath. We met outside the gates of our factory and, loaded with booze, we headed for the delights of the Georgian city. A stop for a drink here and there. All the way, some 12 to 15 miles. Our rations were gone by the time we got there, so a quick visit to a pub for a couple and then an off licence and a sit in the park, before restocking for the journey home. The sun was blazing down and we decided to stop near Saltford, a village on the way back. We were sunbathing by the riverbank where the cycle path crossed on a high bridge some thirty foot above us. The odd pleasure boat went past, cruising the river, but we were unseen in the tall grass on the river's edge. Andy wandered off after having a little swim and the next time we saw him he was stood high above us on the parapet, naked. He picked his spot and leapt into the air. In a flash he hit the water, and we stood up, wondering who was going to finish his drink if he didn't resurface. Andy dragged himself out of the water a few yards from us and said that he had checked out the depth before going up, and what a thrill! Before we went up to match him, he gave us some great advice.

'When you jump off, make sure you hold onto your nuts; mine smacked me in the face when I hit the water.'

I went first and Ken followed. It seemed a lot higher when we stood on the bridge above the water. Luckily, we both followed Andy's advice and looked after the jewels prior to leaping.

When we left that glorious sun trap, we were all the worse for wear and struggled to get the bikes back up and onto the path.

Ken stated that he didn't think he could ride any more and we would have to walk.

'Fuck that, we are only half way. Andy, give me a hand to get Ken on his bike.'

Now Ken is another lad that I have remained friends with to this day. He is an absolutely great guy. He stands around 6ft 4in and carries the lumber to go with it, probably tipping the scales around 18 stone. So you can see our problem…

We managed to get him onto his bike and clip his feet into the pedals.

'Okay, Ken, as we push, you start pedalling.'

'All right, let's go!' he said.

He started off meandering from side to side and we mounted up and followed, much like an escort vehicle following an abnormal load on the motorway.

A couple of times he started to slow and we raced up to him, caught the bike and encouraged him to keep pedalling.

'Keep going, Ken, not too far now.'

Unfortunately, we didn't manage to catch him every time and he toppled off in slow motion. Then we had the hysterical sight of Ken leaning over his bike to put his chain back on and just falling head-first over the bike in the worst gymnastic display ever, with the bike finishing on top of him.

At the time, Ken was living with his parents in Oldland Common, with his then fiancée. This was fortunate, as it meant Andy and I could get him home before we completed our rides home.

Unbeknown to us, Ken was due to go out that evening with the said fiancée, Sharon. To say she wasn't pleased is an understatement. The reader will be pleased to know, though, that they are still married and have two great children, one of which is my godson. So even I was forgiven.

My last abiding memory of that day, though, was when we left Ken he was laid flat out on the sofa with a little Yorkshire terrier basically sat on his face and Ken unable to remove it, just flapping limply away with his hand. Priceless.

Ken and I had adjoining welding booths at work, separated by a large spot-welding machine. Behind that we had a secret shielded compartment big enough to have an upturned tea chest and a chair in it. After the pub most weeks, one or other of us could have a little power nap safe in the knowledge we had the other as an early warning system. Poor old Tommy the foreman.

MORE OF THE SAME

The seasons came and went and the fortunes of Bristol Rovers fluctuated without ever really delivering true success. As the eighties got going, even the support dwindled. Punk rock had arrived in the late '70s and it seemed perfect for the downward spiral we all felt. Eastville was disappearing before our eyes, its dilapidated stands and cold, windswept terracing now there for all to see. As the crowds sank, so did our eternal optimism. But the Gas are ours, and loyalty is by its name steadfast.

Often on a Monday morning, in work after another dismal performance the previous Saturday, we would all bemoan the hopeless feeling we all felt. Working class lads all over the country need something to feel pride in. Our love affair was waning...

'What a load of rubbish again!'

'What the fuck is going on down there?'

'I'll be fucked if I'm going to waste any more of my money watching that lot.'

That was Monday, but Saturday at 12 noon we would still be in the Dirty Duck with the same faces, optimistically waiting for the big win that was inevitably coming. It didn't for a good while, but when it did, it was huge and is still celebrated today.

In the meantime, we kept watching mediocre football in a decrepit but much-loved stadium with less and less fans. We even started to abandon the larger pubs, slinking off to the back street boozers, most notably the Sugar Loaf on St Mark's Road in Easton. It had a jukebox stocked with the music this desperate mob of lost souls wanted to hear: Sex Pistols, The Clash, The Stranglers, and then the light at the end of the darkness – the Jam appeared with great numbers like *In the City* and *This is the Modern World*. The haunting *Down in the Tube Station* struck a chord, and the rawness of Weller's lyrics, along with the smartness of their attire, started to drag us from the despairing melancholy of the punk movement, and only then did we begin to live again.

When punk arrived like a huge battering ram, coinciding with the depressing state of the country, the youth of the day embraced it and rebelled in as shocking a way as each generation can find. The difference with this, as opposed to the '50s and '60s youth, was, unlike previous trends, we were not filled with excitement about the future or even the present. It was despair initially, swiftly replaced by anger.

Drinking in these back street pubs around this time felt depressing, long overdue for a refurb, middle-aged alcoholics propping up the bar or sitting at the rickety mahogany-coloured tables with red velvet seating, pot-marked with circular cigarette burns. The bars were all encompassed by smoke and the smell of tobacco and stale beer.

I took to the music, loving the I-don't-give-a-fuck style, groups like Magazine with *Shot by Both Sides* and the Ruts' magnificent *Babylon's Burning*, The Stranglers and Sham 69 all producing track after track that reflected the dour times we were living in. The Boomtown Rats with *Rat Trap* and The Stranglers' *No More Heroes* were well written and performed songs belying the method of most groups of the time, where they would make one song and disappear forever.

Sham 69 and their West Ham following were playing the Colston Hall, and Rich and I got tickets.

We were only really playing at punks, although we loved the music. Rich dyed his hair green and with our clothes suitably ripped, we got on a bus to town. Two other lads on the bus offended Rich in some way, or maybe it was just in his head – either way, as luck would have it, they got off at the same stop as us. As was the expected norm, we took one each and started a row. The huge bus driver had obviously seen what had started on the bus and took it on himself to separate us all. The objects of our annoyance ran off down the Pithay, a steep little road that ended up near Bridewell Police Station. We took another route, walking down Broad Street in the Old Town towards our big night out, jumping and singing and sweating to the frantic music. We were around ten rows back, and to my joy the support group were Toots and the Maytals, a legendary Jamaican SKA band. As they were finishing their set, I spotted, three rows in front of us, the two lads from the bus. We left it as we really wanted to enjoy the concert. The lead singer, Jimmy Pursey, did his best to rile the crowd by announcing that he knew he was in Bristol because he could see 'some boys wanking in the top row'. This caused an immediate charge towards the stage and, as was common at the time, the first few rows gobbed at the stage and did their best to climb it, but were beaten back by security. Calm was restored and we danced the night away to *When the Kids are United*, *Borstal Breakout* and *Angels with Dirty Faces*. Rich had used vegetable dye to do his hair and he ended up looking like a slimmed-down Hulk with long green streaks running down his face.

When the occasional 'big game' came along, the old guard would return and, through word of mouth, congregate in a more suitable larger pub before the game. Strangely, though, we felt even more dogged in our love of the Gas. They were often referred to as Ragbag Rovers, and now we as fans matched the desperate plight of our club.

But we were still a match for the hated Shitheads across town. Their brief foray into the upper echelons of the Football League had mercifully been brief, and they were now languishing in the same division as us following relegation after relegation to the bottom, and were now returning to the cocky set of supporters I hated with a passion.

'If a City fan was on fire, I wouldn't piss on him,' my brother once said, and I agreed wholeheartedly.

Another derby match came around, away at Ashton Gate, home to the Shit, and as a small group we decided to go for a drink out of the way to avoid getting over-involved. So we headed off up Whiteladies Road, Clifton, and, tucked away in a side street, we settled on the Coach and Horses. Whiteladies Road runs from the top of Park Street, which in turn leads off the centre. It's a long road, home to the BBC studios and countless trendy bars and restaurants. It becomes Blackboy Hill shortly before arriving onto the Downs, a vast green space near the Clifton Suspension Bridge. Clifton, as a whole, is a world away from the inner city areas of town we lived in. It has wealthy people and large impressive homes who live a completely different lifestyle to the vast majority of us.

The pub was a reasonable size on a tarmac square with terraced housing opposite and to the right, with the back yards or gardens of shops and homes to the left. A small walled garden at the front was dotted with no more than four bench-style tables. On the way in I spotted Topper, a Gashead I'd known for some years, and a great lad, tall and broad with cropped hair. He was sat in the 'garden' and we nodded at each other as I entered the bar.

To the right as we approached the bar were some stairs leading up to where the pool table was. We got our drinks and decided on having a game or two. The upstairs room had a few tables and fruit machines, along with a decent pool table. Two windows overlooking the square let just enough light in and we settled in for a few games. Cider, pool, local derby and some mates – the best of days.

The windows were open to allow some air in and the breeze was welcome in the stuffy, dark and creaky room.

After a while we were drawn by shouting or singing coming from outside. At the far end from the left, a large group of City fans came into sight. I looked down and saw Topper and a couple of his mates leap the garden wall and escape down the side of the pub, and who can blame them.

'I never thought to run, when perhaps I should have. Now I couldn't run if I wanted to!'

Colin, no shrinking violet, decided attack was the best form of defence. He grabbed a few pool balls and started launching them out of the window. He never was the sharpest, as they were immediately catapulted back at us. It felt a little bit like being in a pinball machine, with the windows shattering and pictures taking the impact of the salvo. The other thing, though, was that they now knew we were here and we were trapped.

The mob attacked the pub, ascending the stairs. The first thing we greeted them with was a big heavy one-armed bandit pushed into their surprised faces. Their retreat was fast, but only temporary. Then, as a couple of us were still engaged in pool ball tennis at the window, the pool table was dragged over and tipped sideways and utilised as a barrier at the top of the stairs. I snapped my cue in half in order to use it as a club and put it to use on knuckles and faces as they made their assault. We held them off and before long they gave up and fled the pub as the Police arrived to survey the carnage.

Miraculously, once again not one of us suffered any real injuries, apart from a slight cut here and there. We took down the barrier and proceeded to leave. The fruit machine at the bottom of the stairs had been dragged aside and lay prostrate in the middle of the bar area, totally destroyed. 'Thanks, landlord, see you later!' we called out. The landlord didn't look over-impressed.

THE BEAUTIFUL GAME

During all of these turbulent times, when hooliganism was at its zenith, there was, of course, the football. I'm sure that when Rovers were particularly bad – which was a lot – the hunt for confrontation was what kept us interested. It was the only thing that gave us a sense of pride; God knows, the dour spectacle offered on the pitch was nothing to admire. The story of youth fighting each other is as old as the hills – go back in time and the Mods fought the Rockers, Skinheads in the late '60s, Teddy Boys in the '50s; hell, I bet cavemen would have had a row with the Neanderthals in the next valley because they wore different-coloured animal pelts.

The early '70s on the pitch had given us a false dawn, with the likes of Bruce Bannister and Alan Warboys scoring for fun. Smash and Grab this deadly duo were named, and promotion from the Third Division at the end of the '73/'74 season was the reward. The joy was unforgettable, and at last during my time watching them something real to celebrate. The first promotion since 1953, back when there were 'no motorways, mind', and two years earlier my Dad had travelled for eleven and a half hours to get to the FA Cup tie in Newcastle.

It would be another 16 seasons before this could be beaten, but when '89/'90 came around, beaten it would be, in spades.

We survived in the higher league for seven years, never finishing above 15th, and succumbed to relegation back to the old Third Division in

1980/81. The euphoria of being promoted had for many years been replaced with a constant struggle. Depression hung over North Bristol with no end in sight, and the predictable drop left not only the team but the mood of many thousands of Bristolians sinking into an abyss.

Eastville was on its last legs; the long, crooked, wooden Victorian stand was set on fire and burned to the ground: probably by City fans, but never proven. With the stand gone, all there was to see on that side of the pitch were the rears of a row of houses and above that the imposing concrete mass of the M32 Motorway. It seemed the houses had turned their back and the traffic high above couldn't get past fast enough. It always felt cold and windswept, this once-striking stadium with the high-banked open end and oval sand greyhound track circling the pitch. Behind the goals were well-tended flowerbeds; even during the many pitch invasions they were respected and not trampled on, as reported during the rout of Southampton.

Back in the Third Division, we soldiered on. Eventually, finances decided that Rovers could no longer afford the rent to the stadium company and we looked for a new temporary home. True to the name, Bristol ROVERS found it 12 miles away in Bath at Twerton Park. Initially, it was a struggle to come to terms with, but it was a better prospect than ground-sharing with the Shit. We had played a few games there after the fire, but every minute was hated by us and by them, I'm sure.

Moving meant we had to familiarise ourselves with the area and, importantly, the local pubs, of which luckily there were many. Twerton is an area of Bath lacking in all the fine Georgian architecture it is noted for. The ground was just off the A4 as you come in to Bath from Keynsham, a small town on the outskirts of Bristol. All along that stretch of road is a high wall supporting a railway, and access to Twerton Park is under one of a few arches. Boasting tight little streets with terraced houses, it was every bit as scruffy as Eastville, which suited us down to the ground.

It was to be our 'temporary home' for the next 10 years.

Things started to look up: new manager, new ground, new players and better form. Like all football fans, you want your players to give everything, and nothing else is acceptable. If you get beaten by a better team, then so be it, but around this time a team of grit and determination was assembled, led by Ian Holloway, Rovers through and through. Others of note in the late '80s teams were Gary Penrice (like Holloway, a Bristolian), Ian Alexander, David Mehew, Carl Saunders and Devon White (almost Smash and Grab again), and many others who were building to the culmination of something so special in the minds of all Rovers fans that their names just have to be mentioned.

BEYOND ELATION

Finishing eighth in the '87/'88 season, we were again flying in '88/'89, ending the season fifth and missing out on promotion as runner-up in the play-offs. Disappointed, of course, but for the second season in a row we all couldn't wait to get going again.

The new season started well and just got better. I found myself travelling to more away games than ever, and it just kept building. Early in the season we secured a draw across town against City, who were also going well, leading the division for large parts of it. The return game at Twerton was postponed until the last week of the season! Our last two league games were now going to be the Shit at home mid-week and away to Blackpool the following Saturday.

New Year's Eve, and a family gathering at Mum's. The topic, of course, came around to Rovers...

'What do think, Dad? We've only lost two league games all season.'

'Looking good, kid, looking good.'

My brother said, 'City are still going well.'

'Gotta hope they fall along the way.'

'Who we got tomorrow?'

'Away at Rotherham.'

'Fancy going? I'll drive.'

'Yes, why not. Do you think Darrell and Paul might fancy it?'

'I'll call 'em before they get rat-arsed tonight.'

So, in the course of a three-minute conversation, all plans for a big New Year celebration with my wife were cancelled for a trip to Yorkshire in the pouring rain. Surely she'd understand!!! She didn't.

My ex-wife wasn't into football in any way at all and comically she once said, 'You think more of Rovers than you do of me!'

'Well, there's eleven of them,' I replied.

Then she got me back by saying, 'I don't know why you keep going to watch Rovers. They never came to see you when you were bad!'

I, for once, had no reply. I was able to laugh because she was several years late with her statement. We were flying and Saturdays couldn't come around quick enough.

On the way up, we called into my in-laws in the Midlands for a cup of tea. Picture this, my brother and I, along with Darrell, an ex-para with a flat-top haircut, and Paul, a chunky little guy dressed for football in the usual fashionable football gear, sitting in the lounge of my mother-in-law's smart bungalow in a picturesque Midlands village, just outside Burton-on-Trent, and in comes the gold tea trolley with white spoke wheels, loaded with fancies of all description and the best bone-china cups. Would have preferred a mug and some pork pie, but we all behaved impeccably and managed to excuse ourselves after half an hour. Lost 3-2 – typical. On the way to my car, wearing a lovely new leather coat, I had a row with some Yorkshire Tyke, and as we reached the car, I opened the boot and threw the coat in and squared up to him. Dave, Darrell and Paul instantly got ready, but the gobby northerner backed down and scuttled off down the road. I was a little relieved, as the road was absolutely soaking and a long drive sopping wet would not have been pleasant. Maybe the first signs I was growing up! The result wasn't about to spoil our happy new year.

We got to the final week of the league season sitting second, with a record of Won 24, Drawn 15 and Lost only 5 games. We had scored 65 goals and conceded only 35. Trouble was, City were sat in first position, but their form had stuttered.

Fortress Twerton was bouncing like never before, and the local TV cameras were there to record history. If City won, they were promoted as champions. If we won we would go up.

For such a big game I felt nerves, of course, but was also sure that, at last, Rovers would come through and deliver. The Popular terrace was filled to capacity all along the side of the pitch. It seemed everyone in there was willing to do whatever they could to get us over the line. To a man, the whole enclosure was singing and clapping, drowning out the attempts of the red half of Bristol located to our left at the end of the ground. Deliver they did, with a resounding 3-0 win. On the night Rovers were better than them in every department. We had more desire and skill, and from the start of the game I felt the result was never in doubt. The Shitheads were beside themselves and tried to wreck the stadium, ripping out hoardings and throwing them on the pitch. Towards the end of the game, City's manager, Joe Jordan, had gone around to plead to them, trying to restore order, without success. The noise from three sides of this ramshackle stadium was deafening and our chants merciless. We had never had a night like this, but it was only going to be a few more days to wait to see if we could complete the job and be promoted as champions.

The game came to an end and a crescendo of joyous noise flooded Bath. For once, our pitch invasion wasn't in order to attack the other team's fans, but only to show an outpouring of gratitude to this group of determined footballers. We stayed on the pitch for a while and the Reds sloped off, totally dejected. The singing went on long into the night, led by Gerry Francis, the manager, and our wonderful team, legends every one of them.

As much as we wanted to stay and soak it up, my brother Dave and I left in order to get back to our local pub, grab a beer and watch it all again on the TV.

We spent the next few days basking in the glory of promotion and achieving it by outclassing our hated neighbours. Friday arrived and off we went. Dave and I clubbed together and bought enough booze we thought would last the journey. As things turned out, we ended up flogging cans to the others, as they were less prepared than us. The whole of Blackpool seemed to have been rented out by Bristol as en masse we departed north to the tacky seaside town. A bus-load of Kingswood boys and my brother and I, 25 strong, were all booked into a tired but clean hotel just off the seafront, run by the aptly named George and Mildred (well, that's what we named them). We were welcomed like their long-lost children. Arriving on Friday night, this was going to be a weekend to remember.

A large group of the former Tote had taken up residence at the local holiday camp, raising a Rovers flag and getting the traditional Rovers song, *Goodnight Irene*, put onto the jukebox. Around 4,500 made the trip, and some who couldn't get a bed for the night slept where they could. Torquay all over again.

A quick shower and change, then out. We got into a large pub on the front; the bouncers were wary but let us in, along with fans from several other teams who were playing in the North-West on the last day of the season. None of them had the numbers in attendance that we did, though.

The evening was going well, and as we had been drinking constantly since we left Bristol, even having to re-stock around Wolverhampton, some of us were the worse for wear, my brother being one of them.

The music was playing and the dancefloor was so tempting when pissed, and Dave staggered over to dance with a girl. The boyfriend took offence and grabbed my brother, so a little wrestling match started – a little over the top, I felt, so I went over to tidy up. As I got close enough to hide my actions, I delivered a swift uppercut and connected, not unlike the time back in Beachley while marching in the platoon. He fell back and the bouncers were there in a flash.

'Did you see what he did to my brother? I'm not having that.'

'All right, all right, calm down, calm down.'

Very northern, I thought. My brother Dave was ejected, along with the recipient of my punch. I was allowed to stay put. One of the other lads was going back to the hotel, so he accompanied my sibling.

Alan and I, one of the Kingswood boys, sort of got invited to a local club by a couple of girls. **'The older I get, the better I was.'** Come on, Al, we're in here. We raced back to the hotel to get changed into proper going-out gear. When we got back, my brother was sat against the wall in the bar with a pint of lager, with probably just a sip or two taken. He was being entertained by Mildred, although I wasn't sure he was aware of it.

With our tickets for Jokers nightclub in our hands courtesy of the girls, we were off.

We got in. It was a dark, seedy basement club: dark wood, but with nice lighting. It was not unlike every other small ordinary club trying to be the best establishment they could in the constant struggle to attract enough clientele. Entering from the road, we received a warm welcome from the door staff and they swung the door open for us. We descended the central stairs and as we got to the foot we allowed our eyes to adjust for a few seconds. To our left was a long polished brass bar with a multitude of spirits inverted on optics in front of mirrors and glass. The room opened up in front of us and behind, under and around the stairs the club continued with a dancefloor before fading into darkness.

We couldn't see the girls, but more importantly we couldn't see another friendly face. This was a locals place, and already I'd clocked some disapproving glances.

'What do you want to drink?'

'Vodka and Coke; don't think we'll be here long.'

Alan went off to the left to get the drinks and I went off to the right and the toilets. As I got ready to go back out, three lads came in and started the usual rhetoric.

'Got the time, mate?'

'No, sorry.'

'Where you from, mate?'

'You know where I'm from; why you asking?'

They continued to talk crap for a minute or two, obviously trying to build themselves up, but to start with I wasn't biting. Three of them in a tight space – not great odds. Besides, had a game tomorrow I wanted to watch.

After a little bit more of their banality, I just said, '**Look, I'm getting very bored with this. If you aren't going to do anything, get the fuck out of the way.**'

To be honest, I wasn't surprised when they just let me walk out. They were all mouth. Thank fuck for that. It was lucky I left my meeting when I did, because as I did I saw Alan holding a stool and backing out towards the stairs. I quickly got myself a matching bit of furniture and joined him in the retreat.

Towards the top, the stools went flying and we went scampering back to the hotel, giggling like schoolgirls. Didn't even get my Vodka and Coke.

Back in the bar of the hotel, Mildred had gone to bed and left my brother asleep with his beer, which, by the time we got back, still only had a sip taken from it. Up to bed – big day tomorrow.

Blackpool had already been relegated to the Fourth Division, so it was no shock that the attendance at Bloomfield Road that day was probably 5 to 1 in favour of Rovers fans. We had no doubt about the result and another resounding 3-0 win, with the pitch completely surrounded up to the touchline when the third went in, and another mass incursion onto the playing surface delaying the extraordinary celebrations that arrived at the final whistle, with players and officials alike running for all their worth. Our players were trying to reach the tunnel fully clothed for one thing, with souvenirs of kit high on the agenda for some. Promoted as champions ahead of the Shit – what a day! The evening drinking was a blur and we mainly stayed together. There was a visit to the beach, of course, more pubs and back to George and Mildred's to finish the night.

Alan was completely wasted and fell asleep on the floor by the bar. Our hosts had taken themselves to bed, as one of the poor souls had to get up to do our breakfast in the morning. The other lads dragged Alan's trousers down and placed a fan of beer mats into his arse. He never woke up or moved all night. The scream was ear-piercing in the morning when Mildred came down to start work.

Bleary-eyed and hung-over, we all drank champagne before boarding the coach for the long trip back home. With a drinks stop on the way back, we found a pub somewhere north of Birmingham. It was a quiet little village and the rather smart pub was the same. From the car park the entrance had a nice oak-framed porch and the beams continued inside the Olde Worlde inn. Most of us were just grateful to have a bar to lean on and a quiet drink to revive us. Two of the lads decided to have a Bacardi/Vodka drinking race and ordered shot after shot in an attempt to see who could make it to the end of the bottle first. An expensive exercise in a pub when you are paying by the measure. Then another one of us found a pushbike outside and decided to ride it around the inside of the bar. It was just high spirits, as we were still in celebration mode, and although the jovial landlord was patient and accommodating, his relief showed on his face as we thanked him and waved him goodbye. During the long journey home, a couple of the lads were pretty much comatose, and the dreaded razors were used to relieve them of much of their hair from all areas of the body. What a week – and if you read on, you might agree that it's on a par with the end of my story.

Two weeks later, to complete the best season ever, Rovers were making their first Wembley appearance in the final of the Leyland DAF trophy. This was the competition for the lower league teams, and for most the only realistic opportunity to appear at the national stadium.

WEMBLEY, WEMBLEY

I distinctly remember saying when I was younger that the first time I go to Wembley it will be to watch Rovers play. Thank God we got there back then, or I would have missed several great games watching other teams, including England.

Meeting in the car park at Eastville prior to the trip to London, I got talking to Jay, a guy I knew well who over the years had probably made more profit from Rovers merchandise than the club made profit from the actual football. There he was with his stall set up with flags, shirts, hats and wigs, probably some foam hands there as well. The car park was a sea of blue and white, and coaches lined up to transport the thousands of celebrating Gasheads up the motorway.

'This is fantastic, Jay, and you look like you're having a good day,' I said.

'Certainly makes up for the cold, windy Tuesday nights standing on some God-forsaken open end in Oldham or elsewhere,' he said, and we both had a chuckle.

We were playing Tranmere Rovers, and although we would eventually lose the game 2-1, we didn't care. For us it was just a continuation of the carnival-like celebrations of the previous few weeks. The attendance that day was over 48,000, with at least 35,000 from Bristol. The emotions that coursed through me that day from utter joy to immense pride have never left me.

After the unbridled joy of promotion, we settled in to the next couple of seasons of mid-table finishes, the team of heroes were broken up and, predictably, we were relegated the following year.

This was the year the Premier League started, so for that relegation season we were actually then in League Division 1, in name only, of course.

As we got older, it was nice to see the new 'young 'uns' coming through. Never was this more apparent than on an away game to Shrewsbury some years ago.

We arrived in good time and went to a local pub. The pub itself had two distinct bars, one either side of the entrance. My brother and a few mates and I went into the left bar and, as usual at away games, it was full of Gasheads. The unusual thing was, they were all from my generation. In the bar next door it was also full, but this bar had all the young fans in there. A singing competition started and it was like there were two different teams playing; we were singing all the '70s and '80s songs referencing the Tote End and players of the day, and the lads next door – all of whom would never had had the experience of standing there – were singing newer, fresher songs of the day. The one that united both bars was, of course, *Goodnight Irene*.

As the beer flowed, the grown-ups in our bar started to behave like the kids next door. The main thing to do was to keep ducking the brass wall plates being used a Frisbees. I did hear that the flat upstairs got robbed, but no proof, and who knows which bar the perpetrators had come from.

I have said previously that it wasn't all violence and mayhem; we genuinely used to have some real laughs. On another coach trip to Oxford one Boxing Day, we had left the ground with the intention of stopping in Swindon for a drink. During the drive, Charlie and some of the older lads decided everyone was going to get wedged! Now I had a brand new pair of briefs on, a Christmas gift, so I kept my head down for as long as I could. Eventually, with the aisle strewn with the oddest assortment of shredded underwear in both colour and quality, my name was shouted out.

'You've got me, that's mine there!' I said, pointing at nothing in particular.

'Oh, all right then, I think that's the full set.'

'Just imagine,' I said. 'The Old Bill pulls us in and over the radio announces that they have just stopped 50 homosexual football supporters.'

We got to the pub in Swindon and I raced to the toilets, removed my new pants and stuck them in my pocket, just in case the high jinks start again.

Our legendary friend Rod returned from the corridor near the kitchen with huge chunks of Stilton and Cheddar in his hands.

'Trolley-load of it out there – go and help yourself.'

We all did; even the grapes went, along with the crockery.

On the way back from another trip, we stopped in Wootton Bassett and held an impromptu kangaroo court.

The defendant was charged with two offences. One of which was that during a coach trip to Port Vale earlier in the season, he did engage in sexual activity with one of the girls on the coach. The girl in question was a large girl, to say the least, with a pink fringe and debateable morals. I knew this girl and she used to use the same local Chinese as me. One night I was in there and I swear she ordered the menu and had pie and chips while she waited for it to be cooked.

Maff was the Judge, and after not very much deliberation and statements from key witnesses, the judgment was delivered.

'How do you find the defendant on the first charge of running from the City?'

Maff: 'GUILTY!'

'And how do you find the defendant on the second charge of shagging Fat Sheila?'

Maff: 'VERY GUILTY!'

The pub erupted and a suitable forfeit was pronounced.

ROVERS RETURN

We left Twerton Park to return back to our heartland at the end of 1996. Our new home, initially as tenants to Bristol Rugby Club, was at The Memorial Stadium at the top of Muller Road. Slap bang in Rovers Territory, with the Gloucester Road and its plethora of drinking establishments, it promised to be a good and vital move.

It was right that we were returning, but I had a strange feeling of loss at leaving Bath. The ground had been good to us, saved us from possible extinction and gave every Gashead the most memorable night of our lives.

It didn't take long for the 'tenancy agreement' to change; with both clubs on a financial tightrope, a deal was struck to preserve the stadium in the event of one or other entering dire straits. This happened, fortunately for us, to the Rugby Club, and the result of the turmoil was that Bristol Rovers finally, after around 60 years, once again owned our own ground. The Rugby Club continued to play here for a while, but now ply their trade at Ashton Gate. Rather sad, as the Memorial Stadium was dedicated to the players and staff of the Rugby Club that fell in the First World War.

The upshot of it all, though, was now we could play on a decent pitch, with the grass cut to the right length.

The big disappointment for me was that I no longer lived in Bristol; after travelling to Bath to watch games, I was still having to travel to watch them in my home town. A few years earlier, around the end of 1990, I was made redundant from the factory where I had worked for 13 years. My wife was made redundant at the same time at her work, so with a mortgage to cover we had to think of something to do. I had always worked part-time in pubs and clubs, and my wife was a brilliant cook, so we decided the licensed trade could get us both employed at the same time.

We joined a small independent brewery from Dorset and after some training we began to manage pubs. We started our training period not too far away in Nailsea, at the Old Farmhouse.

At the time the pub was occasionally used by some City players, and as hard as I tried to be professional, I couldn't contain my contempt, making them fully aware of my allegiance. One particular night there were a few of them in, including their goalkeeper. When he dropped his glass, I erupted with laughter, asking him what chance he'd have with a ball if he couldn't hold on to his drink. I seem to remember he had a sense of humour failure – oh, well!!!

Accommodation was provided in a two-bedroom stone cottage in the car park. We began in January 1991 and quickly realised that the cottage had no heating whatsoever. The fireplace in the lounge would not have looked out of place in a dolls house. One of my first duties in the morning was to chop kindling and gather logs for the pub's fires. The logs were stacked outside the cottage, and I would have to put the kindling into the oven in our kitchen in order to dry them out. On our break after lunch, my wife and I would just get back into bed fully clothed in order to stay warm. The work was relentless and we would only get one full day off a week. We would often drive to Bristol on these days to visit Ken and Sharon at their home in Kingswood. They were now married and expecting their first child. As always, we would be welcomed and offered a cup of tea as we sat on the sofa. By the time the refreshing brew arrived, both my wife and I would be out-for-the-count asleep. Ken and Sharon would quietly slip out of the room and leave us to rest. We had progressed well during training, as after three months we were transferred to another pub not far from Reigate in Surrey. We went one way and two couples went the other. The manager there had been relatively successful, but unbeknown to us had tendered her resignation and we were brought in with the intention of taking it on. We continued training for a further two months and amazingly while there our living accommodation had gotten worse. From the freezing stone cottage we were now living in a mouldy old caravan. The door was so old that we had to lock it with a padlock. At least we were tucked away around the back with a field in front of us. The manager left and we were at least then able to move into the flat above the pub. This first appointment became so successful, but at a cost. Our relationship faltered through the sheer commitment we offered the job, working six and a half days a week, extremely long hours and moving away across the country for the privilege.

When I could manage to get away, I would have to pick and choose the games I could attend. Games in London were favoured, so I rarely missed one of those. In every pub I ran, the customers were made aware very quickly who I supported, and those who I got on well with occasionally came to games with me. One particular friend I still talk to was born on the Mile End Road and was a big West Ham fan. Another supported Crystal Palace, and if they came to Rovers games I would also go to Selhurst Park or The Boleyn (Upton Park) with them. One year, Rovers were actually playing at West Ham, so we got as many tickets as possible and around 15 from my pub went to the game, some in with the West Ham fans and the rest of us in with the Gas. Dave, the Hammer fan, ended up with us. Julian Dicks, son of an ex-City manager, was playing and scored in a 3-0 win for West Ham. Dave managed to control his joy and I hid my disappointment. It showed, though, how times were changing. In the early years I would not have been able to have him sat next to me, friend or not. We all went for a curry on the Barking Road after, and as we were all starting to order, Dave spotted two religious sisters looking through the window at the menu. Quick as a flash, he called the waiter and said, 'I asked for two Naans, mate!'

The move back home for Rovers was not to be a catalyst for better times. Even a highlight of reaching the play-off after finishing fifth, we took a 3-1 lead into the second leg and lost 3-0. To make matters worse, City got promoted out of our division. The inevitable came around in the new millennium (2000/2001) and we were relegated again.

***

We were a charitable bunch in the pub. Nestled in an affluent area of the country, we would host regular events for good causes. Every year the company I worked for would donate a good amount of money for a fireworks display. This in itself was great for me as it got me out from behind the bar and given a chance to relive my childhood. Companies from miles around would donate pallets and any burnable waste items. We always had to wait until the last day to erect it and would use a JCB from a local farm. The reason wasn't due to kids, like when we were young, but a travellers' site about a mile away. We would spend the day in the paddock by the side of the pub, assembling Mount Vesuvius and digging holes for the mortars. One year we even had a huge laser show with skips full of water and a huge scaffold assembled. We had to inform Gatwick, as we were close to the flight path. That was the year I managed to get the village's most famous celebrity to introduce the evening's entertainment. Showbiz royalty Dame Judi Dench and her husband Michael Williams graced us with their presence on an absolutely filthy night as the heavens opened with a torrential downpour. Our spirits weren't dampened, as like schoolkids we went about launching the fireworks. Someone, though, managed to load some 4-inch mortars into the 6-inch tubes; the result was they exploded around 12ft from the ground. It was like a scene from the film *Apocalypse Now* as we all scattered and dived for cover.

The most exciting thing we decided to do was a parachute jump. This was to be in aid of a local charity called the Winged Fellowship. There was a huge house a couple of miles up the road and the Fellowship offered holidays for disabled young people. This afforded some respite for their full-time carers. Over the years I had managed to get a bar installed there, courtesy of our company, which was particularly welcomed by the manager, Pete, who loved the bitter we sold. Eight of us travelled to Diss in Norfolk late in summer for the weekend. Training on Saturday and the leap of faith on the Sunday. I mentioned at the time that for me to get a weekend off in August I would have jumped without a parachute. The group consisted of four younger lads, including a representative from the charity, a great lad called Billy from Birmingham and a potential Zulu Warrior in the making. Skinhead and wiry, he hailed from the Kings Norton area. The rest of the party were all in their early 30s; this included Dave and myself.

We arrived in the great flatlands of Norfolk and checked into a local hotel, before arriving for the training. We were doing a static line jump, which means you are not strapped to another person. You are connected by a line to the aircraft and as you jump, after a little freefall, the line pulls the 'chute and deploys it automatically. So you really have to listen to what's being said. Jumping off tables and screaming 'One thousand, two thousand, three thousand, check canopy.' Then, of course, according to the state of the 'canopy', you either thanked God that all was well, or you had to decide how the fuck you were going to survive. The sort of malfunctions that can happen are that the cells of the square parachute have not fully inflated, in which case you carry out a push-pull action on the 'risers' – those are the lines you are connected to the canopy with. If that doesn't work and you are still plummeting to earth at a rate of knots, or you have a 'line over' – this is where the risers are over the canopy, preventing inflation – there is only one option. No, not panic – but I'm sure that happens. You have to deploy your reserve 'chute, but first get rid of the old one. It must take a brave man or woman to do that. After a good couple of hours of familiarisation, we were released with the warning that if anyone smelled of alcohol in the morning, they would not be permitted to jump.

Saturday night, and after an evening meal, the younger lads retired to pray in their rooms. The older group thought bollocks to that, we could die tomorrow – and hit the bar. We all had enough to aid the fitful sleep we were all destined to have that night and reluctantly went to bed.

Full English the next morning – what else for your last meal? – and off we went to the airfield. During the Saturday briefings somebody asked, 'When we jump out, what sort of area are we looking at to get our bearings?' Very good, I thought, I was just about to ask that myself!!!!

The instructor laid a 3ft by 4ft map on the floor and stood on it. Pointing down, he said, 'That's all you need to look for.' The landing zone was quite distinct, as it was a huge pentagon-shaped field of wheat. Should be simple enough, I thought.

'Oh, another thing,' continued our instructor. 'If you think you're going to hit a building, try and turn sideways as you hit it. It will do less damage.'

'To us, or the building?' someone predictably piped up.

We were fitted with the parachutes and helmets with radios, although we had been told they didn't work very well. We then had to wait our turn. The queue for the toilets was around the corner. Grown men were finding a little quiet spot to gather their thoughts and perhaps have a little word with the big man upstairs. If they waited a while, I thought, they could talk when they were a little closer.

The wind got up and we were informed that if it was above 15 knots we couldn't jump. After all the build-up, we wanted to jump. The aircraft was a small Cessna with the wing over the roof, and no door on the side to enable the exit. Only three or four at a time could jump, and Dave was called along with a couple of the other lads. We all walked out from the hangar to watch.

His jump went well enough, but another guy on the plane swore that as he went out his arm came back in, trying to grab anything at all to save himself. Dave himself reckoned his arse bit off a bit of the fuselage as he was waiting for the call to jump. Billy was on the same flight and he was unfortunate to have twisted lines, which meant that the canopy couldn't fully open. He had to push his risers out to encourage the lines to untwist. He was descending a little quicker than desired, but he managed to sort it all out and you could hear the relief as he continued to earth. Lucky he went to bed early last night, we all thought.

My turn came, and as my name was called out over the tannoy, my stomach churned. Four of us walked to the tiny single-engine plane and boarded. I was last on, which meant that I would be sitting by the open door next to the pilot and subsequently I would be first to jump. The line was connected to an anchor point behind the pilot's chair. I was sat facing the rear of the aircraft with the pilot to my right. The Jump-master was directly in front of me, all the seats were removed and everyone was sitting on the floor. Behind him were the other three sacrificial lambs. I hoped I didn't look as nervous as them. As the plane taxied down the grass runway, the noise drowned out everything else. On the front of the parachute packs we all had an altimeter. We were going to 3,500ft, so I kept my eye on it as we climbed. The drone of the engine continued up through some clouds and I tried to keep a view of our landing zone.

As we reached altitude, the pilot throttled back and the hum of the engine diminished. Looking at the Jump-master, he nodded and indicated for me to get ready to go. My stomach did cartwheels again as I then needed to dangle my left leg out of the plane, lift my right leg over the Jump-master's legs and then pivot around until I was facing the direction we were travelling in. Half in, half out of the plane.

'This must be when Dave's arse started chewing the plane,' I thought.

Looking out at the wing just above eye level, it had been plastered in gaffer tape. Luckily, I didn't think I would need to duck. After waiting what seemed like an age, I was given the instruction to go. Pushing myself out and not remembering the one thousand chant at all, I just made a roar of resignation. After a few seconds I felt a reassuring tug and looked up; the plane was already disappearing and a large billowing canopy came into view to cosset me back to terra firma. I gave a huge shout of relief and then set about enjoying the flight. First things first: find my bearings. I looked out in front of me and didn't recognise anything. On these square parachutes there are levers to pull to change direction and also to pull both at the same time to flare the canopy when landing. So I pulled the right pulley and turned towards it, still not recognising the landscape. Shortly before I started to panic, wondering if I had been blown miles off course, I remembered to look straight down. I was exactly over the hangar, approaching the five-sided field. The radio crackled in my helmet and I was given instructions for my approach. This wonderful experience was coming to an end all too soon and I landed like many before me, when the 'ground rush' makes you think you are lower than you actually are. I stepped onto the ground fully three foot before I should and landed in a crumpled heap.

DARK DAYS

Along with the breakdown of my relationship with my wife, the pressure of work had become so great that one night I found myself stood over the parapet of a bridge over the M23 motorway. My intention was to jump. Life had become a struggle of ridiculous hours of work, and even though my wife and I were still together, a great feeling of loneliness haunted me. Every day was the same: get up really early in order to start the day's chores. Hours of work before we even opened the doors to customers. After the lunchtime rush, I would try to get an hour's break if I wasn't rostered on. Even when on the 'break' I would never take my shoes off and I would keep looking out of the upstairs window to count the cars. If there were a certain number, I would be back down. Never getting to bed before 1am and up at 6am wasn't sustainable. Even when I went to bed I would fall asleep almost instantly, but wake up within an hour and then watch the moon travel across the window frame. My default setting of humour saved me that night on the bridge. As I looked down, I thought, 'Fuck me, that's a long way down.'

I got back into my car and sat trembling for 20 minutes before I was able to drive home. I must have looked shocking, because my wife said so. I confessed what had happened and she immediately showed the compassion I knew she had. I was in front of my doctor the next day and referred to a specialist at the local hospital. Diagnosed as clinically depressed, I then began the long process of recovery. I had a break from work when I was taken off to Norfolk for a couple of weeks and spent my days on my own, cycling the countryside and stopping for pub 'lunches'. I was also prescribed a drug which required weaning onto and off. In a quiet moment I read the comprehensive list of possible side effects, which included a loss of appetite and dry mouth. After some weeks I had a routine meeting with my female doctor and she enquired how the tablets were working. By this time I was feeling much more positive and my sense of humour which had saved me on the bridge resurfaced.

'They seem to be working well, I'm feeling better by the day.'

'Oh, well, that's very positive, but you must keep on them, at least for the foreseeable future. They need to correct the clinical imbalance.'

'I will, thank you, but I am worried about one of the stated side effects.'

'Which one in particular, Stephen?'

'Well, Doctor, it does say that they could delay ejaculation… I think three months is taking the piss a bit. But having said that, can I have a few boxes for my mates?'

The young doctor blushed slightly but smiled, saying, 'Well, there has been an improvement in your demeanour. I'm very pleased, and keep taking the tablets.'

The signs that I was getting ill were there long before my third attempt at flying off that bridge. A friend of mine who used the pub named Hadyn, a stocky former boxer and talented singer, was also a salesman with a gift of the gab. He was at the time selling copier machines, but had previously sold timeshares on the Costas. I was looking for a route out and we were both about to go into selling Spanish timeshare in Russia. All arranged and flights booked to Ekaterinburg in the Siberian wasteland, I bought the biggest, warmest coat I could find and gave my notice to the brewery. No thoughts for my wife or the consequences. It was, of course, a cry for help, and fortunately my depression was diagnosed before we left. As luck would have it, the whole thing was cancelled as the Russian government shut down the existing offices, stating they did not want foreigners selling foreign property to Russian citizens. Earlier we had taken a short holiday to Tunisia together and were discussing the move to Russia; apparently, we were to be supplied with a driver/bodyguard and a housekeeper. Settling on Igor as the name of our phantom bodyguard, we both decided the maid would be called Olga Onyerbacyabitch. Giggling away like naughty schoolboys on the plane, we attracted some very disapproving glances.

Although fully recovered from this hidden illness, there are still days when for no apparent reason I can feel myself sinking into the abyss of hopelessness that I experienced all those years ago. Fortunately, I recognise these dark days as they were once described to me and I am now able to reflect on things and recover without too many issues.

Towards the end of our time in Surrey, word had spread around the villages that we were leaving, and on one of the final nights the pub was packed and one of my local customers came to me and asked if I could do something about some young lads that kept trying to start a fight. He pointed them out and I went to have a chat. Looking around, it became apparent that there were around 10 in the group. I started to talk to them and immediately the gobby leader started saying, 'You don't remember me, do you?'

Without a pause, he pressed on, saying I had barred him and his mates a few years earlier, when they were 15 or so. He was obviously here as he knew I was leaving and his intentions were clear. Not wishing to linger in conversation with the cocky fucker, I just said, '**Guess what, you're still barred, so on your way, and take all your little gang with you.**'

'You can't get me out of here.'

Still aware of his mates, who were all sitting up like meerkats, I just said that I thought I could, and quickly pulled his arm towards me and across his body. Reaching over with my other arm, I grabbed him in a stranglehold and I managed to tie him up and we headed for the door. The door of the pub was a square porch with the inner door swinging to the right as you go through it and the main heavy front door opening the other way. This was always pegged open while we were open. As we reached the first door, his gang of followers were on their feet, heading to assist. He managed to get his arms free and placed them not unlike a tripod against the pillars either side of the door. Looking over his shoulder, he sneered, 'Told you, you can't get me out of here.'

'**And I told you I could.**'

At the same time, I delivered a swift left hook up and under his ribs. He collapsed into the doorway and I followed him, along with several of the gang. My arms were trapped, and as I was struggling to free them, I saw a sovereign-ringed fist flying over the top. Catching me on the left eyebrow, it split the skin perfectly. I managed to release my left arm and using the flat of my hand, I was able to ram the culprit's head hard against the lovely big black door knocker. Our mouthy troublemaker fell unconscious out of the pub and all of his entourage grabbed the limp body and dragged him away into the night. Instantly, my eye socket turned all shades of blue and the blood started a meandering trickle down the left side of my face. It was the first time I had been cut by a punch, and it really annoyed me. My more respectable clientele showed their appreciation, and after a little first aid, I enjoyed the supply of complimentary drinks – for medicinal purposes, of course.

A NEW CHALLENGE

We moved pubs in 1997, moving to a brand new purpose-built house in Hampshire. One of my first thoughts when offered it was: great, closer to home; I can get to some home games now.

The pub was a roaring success, but the cracks in our relationship were still there. My wife and I separated, although we remained on good terms, citing the business as the principal reason. I continued to run this house for over five years and, unbeknown to me, had already interviewed my future wife while recruiting staff for this new venture.

The business was a first for the company that usually operated country pubs or houses in rural market towns, with the exception of a sprinkling of houses in London. The concept was for a country house on the edge of town. It proved to be so successful, the company repeated the model time and time again. It took off, taking more cash and turning a greater profit than almost every other house in the group. This afforded me, as a single manager, more freedom. I had an assistant manager and started taking Saturdays as my day off. Again, some of the customers became friends and started attending games with me. Indeed, around this time I was even able to get a season ticket, as I knew I could get to the majority of games.

Two lads from this pub were regular travellers with me. One, Adam, has sadly passed away now, but he was a great softly spoken man around 6ft. The other was Clive, another tall member of what the

A NEW CHALLENGE

bar staff secretly called the Sad Bastards Club. These were the lonely divorcees who propped up the end of the bar nightly. Clive was in his 40s and still living at home, and, after a brief marriage, to my knowledge still does.

A good day was promised when Rovers were drawn away to Derby County not long after they had moved into their new Pride Park Stadium. Adam, in his normal fashion, said, 'I'll drive and you can have a drink with your mates.'

We decided to share the driving – me up, him back!!! And after a Full English and a pint, we set off early. Fifteen minutes later, on a quiet weekend morning with a clear motorway, I reached a decent speed. Then I saw a Volvo approaching from behind at warp speed. It was then I noticed the little blue lights flashing in the grille and pulled over.

In the wing mirror, after I have pulled up, I saw the tallest gangly plod strolling towards me.

'Hurry up, for fuck's sake, we've got a game to go to!'

'Have you got your licence with you?' he sneered.

'No, I don't believe I do.'

'Well, you're not going to have it for much longer. Come with me.'

I got out and walked to his car.

'Get in there.' He pointed at the passenger door.

I sat down and noticed he had a lovely picture of my car on his monitor.

'You went past me at 115mph two miles back and I've just caught up with you.'

Want to get yourself a faster car, I thought to myself. I tried being civil, mentioning the football and the clear conditions, etc, but he was having none of it.

I hadn't realised that he hadn't pushed some button or other to calibrate and find the true speed over a set distance, or whatever it is they needed to do. I was aware, though, that anything over 100mph carried a ban of some sort, so imagine my relief when the calibration showed 99.7mph. He was absolutely gutted and spluttered out, 'Well, you can take a fine and points or go to court.'

'Well, thank you, officer. I'll take the fine this time I think.'

Paperwork done, and as soon as I was out of sight I got back up to cruising speed. Problem was, we didn't arrive at the Navigator pub until 11am and there were about 100 thirsty Gasheads waiting to get in.

Derby's grey-headed Italian striker Fabrizio Ravanelli scored, but the latest in a long line of goalscorers Rovers had managed to unearth, Nathan Ellington (The Duke) hit three for a wonderful win. Adam drove us home and we finished the day at my pub, celebrating long into the night.

The year 2000 and approaching my 40th birthday. As I am writing this, I'm staring down the barrel of my 60th, and if I tried to recollect every event I would be writing well into retirement.

A NEW CHALLENGE

Four days before my 40th birthday I became a grandfather for the first time. I was chuffed to pieces and was still celebrating on my birthday, when a big party had been arranged, including a coachload from Bristol. The driver was useless and went the wrong way, not arriving until gone 9pm. On the bus were my parents, close friends and family and a good selection of Bristol Rovers' finest, including Rod and several of the Kingswood boys.

The pub was a large building with two entrances either side of a big, wide seating area with floor-to-ceiling glass. The building was thatched and we had parking for over 80 cars. If you entered via the left-hand door the bar was to the right along the far wall. To the left was predominately a seating area. Thatched roof and no jukebox or pool table, it was a destination pub but with a large regular drinking clientele.

Some time earlier, one of my old mates from Kingswood who I had known since I was 14 had got me to enter a raffle for a signed shirt, but said if he won it, he would give it to me, as long as I got it framed and put up in the pub. Of course he won it and £200 later it had been framed and given pride of place in the bar area.

Steve, the old friend, wasn't on the coach, but had stayed in a local hotel for the evening with some others and their wives. After the happy birthdays, the first question was, 'Where's the shirt?' I was so pleased to be able to show him.

As the coach party tumbled out and into the pub through the middle door amid a rowdy whirlwind of noise, I watched as all the locals melted away from them towards the top end of the pub. Only Adam and Clive stepped forward to greet them. Friends from all stages of my life were there, and on the whole they were self-policing. The mother of one of my locals did mention to a friend, though, that, 'One of those lads has got his penis out.'

'What is it like?' came the reply.

'Well, it's quite large, actually!!'

I never congratulated Colin on his display, it's just not the sort of thing you do, and although great to see him there, it was a relief when he collapsed back onto the coach.

The evening ended with customers and family and friends mixing quite happily, and all were encouraged to join in the rousing rendition of *Goodnight Irene* before the coach departed. Those remaining continued long into the early hours.

Another highlight of my time at this pub harked back to the charity events I had been involved in during the five years in Surrey. Some bright spark suggested we should perform the Full Monty for Comic Relief. Christ, I thought, the parachute jump was frightening. In honour of the pub name, we were going to perform the Full Pompey...

There were six of us, including Clive and an even older guy called Roger. The instigator of the whole event was 'Jingle', who liked nothing more than showing off. The troupe was made up with Andy, a tall builder type, and another younger barman, Dan.

We decided to do two numbers and set about rehearsing for three weeks in my lounge. Another regular, Kath, helped to make all the costumes, and was also responsible for the stage curtains, while her son sorted the lighting. We had T-shirts made to sell and advertise the event. Interest quickly escalated, and so did our nerves.

The stage was set up in the raised section slap bang in front of the bar. The limit on seating was around 130, and on a busy Friday with standing at the bar there could be around 180 inside the building. I decided early on, due to the interest shown, that we needed door staff on to limit the attendance for safety reasons.

Rehearsals had gone well and for the first number, *You Sexy Thing* by Hot Chocolate, we would be wearing cut-off jean shorts, boots, a white vest and hard hats. We were all upstairs and you could hear the crowd buzzing. Over 270 had managed to cram into the building – so much for the door control. All the bar staff had collected beer crates to stand on. We had no way to get to the stage via the planned route and had to walk out of the back of the building and back in through the kitchen to get around eight foot closer than the original route. Luckily, another of my mad locals, Jim, had dressed in a short figure-hugging red dress, complete with red nose, and he led us through the swarm of people. Most of us had had a few vodkas or Jack Daniels to settle the nerves. We had expected the place to be full, of course, but hoped it would be mainly females. Not the case, as the demographic was worryingly even. The music died as our compère welcomed everyone and reminded them all of the good cause we were here to support. He then introduced us all individually and collectively as The Full Pompey, a play on the name of the pub, The Portsmouth Arms. The curtain was raised and the familiar song began – the song we had heard 100 times in my lounge – and like six rank amateurs, we attempted to entertain the strangest stripper audience ever.

Off we went into the routine that had been drilled into us. At a specific point in the song we all had to rip the vests off, and we did so to howls of not quite sure delight, but the punters were participating fully in the evening. Then, secretly hidden in our short pockets, out came little bottles of baby oil. We all squirted our chests and massaged away, and it fell on Jingle and I to walk to two pillars and gyrate up and down. Later, back in the lounge, I mentioned that someone was giving it large rubbing my leg when we were at the post. My partner shouted, 'That was me!'

'The older I get, the better I was.'

As the number finished, no more clothing was removed – we wanted them begging for more, of course! We all picked up a red rose to hand to a member of the audience as we left the stage. As a laugh, I handed mine to another mate I had spotted there, James, who accepted it with an embarrassed grin.

Back upstairs, another couple of rounds were delivered from the bar and thrown back quickly. We now changed, ready for our big number: *What a Feeling*, by Irene Cara. Kath helped us very enthusiastically into our bowties, white shirts and trousers, all complete with Velcro fastening.

The introductions were repeated and the pub erupted with applause and cheers. They were easily pleased – the Chippendales had nothing to fear.

The song started slowly and we all moved around to the choreography, changing positions on the stage and then forming a line. The bowties were unfastened and spun in our hands, before releasing them into the baying audience. The number built and the shouts of 'Get 'em off' rose. The shirts were ripped away at different times; all planned, of course. One of us didn't manage to release the complete shirt, being left with a trailing sleeve for a few seconds. Standing sideways on again, our belts were slid from the waist and dropped to the floor. A little more posturing and strolling around the stage. We formed up towards the end of the number, with me at the end of the line. The noise was deafening, while the bar staff had refused to serve a drink throughout the performance. A video camera had captured the whole show and the final important part was upon us. We all in synchronicity turned away from the thronging mass. Precisely on time, we yanked the trousers and they came away beautifully. The crowd cheered as we are stood facing away, dressed only in G-strings.

A dramatic pause and we all turned to reveal large red noses on the front of the G-strings. All of us, except me, that is. I had a little tiny one and the other five all leant over to look sympathetically. The curtain fell and Kath raced behind and quickly produced another little laugh for the audience. As an encore, which was called for by the appreciative crowd, we were all now draped in towels. As one, we turned away and dropped them to reveal written on our buttocks COMIC RELIEF. The whole evening and subsequent donations raised over £3,000.

It wasn't always good fun and good causes. Some people just couldn't behave, and over the years I have had to get a few drunk or violent customers out in the interests of the general public. Keeping calm is the first rule. Being positive and showing determination also helped. Sometimes the physical match-up favoured me, but one incident in my pub in Surrey could have ended very badly for me.

One busy lunchtime I was at the food counter taking orders for lunches from the many business clientele we used to attract. The bar was a sort of horseshoe shape with the front of house hidden from me by the back of the bar. Anna, a lovely young girl who worked full-time for me at lunchtimes, was serving at the front and she came around to me looking quite stressed. She said there was a man being abusive and who had pushed another customer out of the way. I took a quick look and saw the man in question was well over 6ft tall, around 30 years of age and very broad. I was in the middle of changing a barrel of bitter and the dregs of the previous keg were in a glass on the bar. He picked it up and downed the lot.

I was thinking, 'If I've got to tackle this bloke, he may well rip my head off and drop the empty glass down my neck; but at least he might shit himself on the way home.' This cheered me up somewhat.

I had a word over the bar with him, which had no effect on his behaviour at all. He did stagger away towards the front door and I decided I would just try and go in low in a rugby tackle style and force him through the door and out onto the garden. I would then attempt to deal with whatever came next.

As I made my way towards certain death, my wife was delivering a couple of meals to a table near to where he was standing. As she passed him he spat onto one of the plates. My wife hit the roof in her middle class way, shouting, 'HOW DARE YOU BEHAVE IN THAT MANNER IN MY PUB!'

I swear to God, this huge beast that a minute or two ago wanted to kill me and everyone else in the vicinity actually apologised to her. He left the pub swearing, slammed the door and punched the reinforced wire glass panel, smashing it for good measure. He then proceeded to jump up and down on a bench before disappearing across some fields. For my part, I breathed a sigh of relief. This is just an example of how you had to put yourself on the line in the interests of your customers and business.

The most satisfying times were when you could resolve an issue without actually having to physically throw people out.

At the Surrey pub I was having some issues with a local lad who thought he was the dog's bollocks. During our conversation regarding his imminent departure from the establishment, he informed me that he was 'The hardest bloke around here.'

With my best poker face on, I said to him, **'That may be true, but I'm not from around here!'**

A good old bit of front and he left without another word.

Christmas time could be particularly tricky. The first Christmas we were at the new pub in Hampshire and it was Christmas Eve. As was normal during the afternoon, I would regularly have around 20 to 30 local builders or window fitters in. Of course, on the day before Christmas the spirits were high. Most afternoons the place would be quite lively with all that goes with it. There was, however, an unwritten law that after five the language would be tempered as other customers would start to arrive. This arrangement usually worked well, but at Christmas some have a little too much and find it difficult to control themselves. One guy in particular was using the full set of profanities and getting louder by the minute. I let him know that he would have to calm down. He acknowledged me and apologised. Ten minutes later I had to speak to him again. This time he was not quite so compliant, so I told him he needed to leave. He nodded, but offered a few choice words as he started to walk along the bar to the far door.

Keeping my eye on him, I managed to serve a customer and then noticed he had stopped and was talking to some more of the crowd. I could hear all the f's and c's again, so I walked around the bar and went up to him, close to his mates.

'I asked you to leave, and you are still here. Now I am telling you to leave,' I said.

'Fuck you, let's go outside,' he slurred.

'Okay, after you.'

He seemed a little surprised by my readiness to go with him, and he spun around and staggered to the door. I duly followed him out and he unsteadily turned to face me.

At this point, I leant forward and said, '**Listen to me, this is what's going to happen. You are going to swing a punch at me and miss. Then I am going to put you flat on your arse. Why don't you just go home and enjoy Christmas?**'

His befuddled mind computed what I had just said and then he nodded and trotted off, wishing me a Merry Christmas as he went.

Years earlier, I would not have taken the time to explain what was going to happen, just enjoyed watching him find out for himself. But this was every bit as satisfying. His only crime was being completely pissed, and I had let him have his moment in the spotlight with his mates, not losing face. Most importantly, the business didn't suffer. His 'mates', I discovered as I went back in, were as relieved as me to have seen him go home.

MAYBE I NEED TO GROW UP

My new football buddies were travelling with me to games regularly. Clive especially enjoyed the days out. Living away from Bristol, it was difficult staying in touch with people and to be able to travel with them to away games. So, often it was Clive, Adam and myself. It wasn't the same; we normally drove, so the drinking had to be watched. All in all, it became more civilised. I guess not a bad thing, as I was now in my 40s. We had driven to the likes of Peterborough, Brentford, Gillingham, Barnet, and all down the east side. On the days we would come to Bristol for the home games, occasionally we'd book a hotel and spend the night out in town.

Clive and I decided to take in a game at Cardiff. Train was the obvious route, so off we went for a drink-fuelled marathon with changes at Salisbury and a stop in Temple Meads. With the time it was going to take, we left very early. After Salisbury, the train was picking up Gasheads at every stop, and the atmosphere was building and the cider was flowing. At Temple Meads, hundreds more joined our jolly boys' outing and we all looked forward to a great day out. As we pulled into Cardiff and alighted from the train in full voice, we were then met by several Robocops: the South Wales Constabulary in full riot dress addressed their visitors.

MAYBE I NEED TO GROW UP

'Right, boys,' said Robocop 1 in his best singy-songy accent, 'we are going to take you to a pub now, and you will all stay there. If you wander off, you will fucking get what's coming to you, right?'

'Do you work for the tourist board, mate?' piped up one.

'Welcome to Wales,' shouted another, and then a chorus of 'There will be a welcome in the hillside', cut short by a united chant of 'England, England, England'.

We were escorted through the streets of Cardiff and deposited in a large pub in the shadow of the Millennium Stadium. It was heaving with Bristol boys and a volatile atmosphere was building, courtesy of our welcoming party and the massed ranks of Police circled outside.

It was a warm day, so a good few were outside drinking on the pavement/road under the watchful eye of our guards. At the ends of the streets in both directions, Cardiff fans were gathering, and we were waiting for their move. The pub's main bar had a Juliet balcony around three foot off the ground, and the doors were wide open to allow some air into the packed room.

In the men's room, a basin and toilet bowl had been ripped out and thrown onto the urinal. Water was flooding the area. I got another drink and Clive and I stood outside. Then, some bottles and rocks were thrown by the Cardiff boys and instantly the charge to get to them was on. Breaking the Police line was ineffective, and they instantly pushed back, hitting out with their nightsticks. I was standing against a tall window of the pub as one of the South Wales officers stuck his truncheon up under Clive's throat and pushed. The pair of them were across the road in no time, and the disorder continued, with Rovers fans trying to get at the Cardiff boys, who, knowing we couldn't break the overzealous boys in blue, got closer and the barrage of bricks continued. The Juliet balcony was rammed and pushed and eventually gave way, ripping clean out of the brickwork, and a fountain of Gasheads tumbled out onto the pavement, and at the same time the window I was still stood under exploded in a shattering shower of glass as a chair was thrown through it. The attempts to break the cordon gathered momentum and from the Police point of view reinforcements arrived in the nick of time. The beatings around the legs continued as the chaotic scene threatened to turn into a full-scale riot. Order was restored from the strong-arm Tactical Support Group. The pub was in no condition to continue serving, and I was sure the staff were mightily relieved when we were all escorted away to the ground.

After our day out to Cardiff – truncheon up the throat and being showered with glass aside – another opportunity for a good day arose. Swindon away!

We would have to change in Reading but that's just a chance for another drink, great.

Off we set. I had spoken to some lads in Bristol and knew we were meeting in the Rifleman pub in Swindon town centre. I hadn't been in there since we ate all the cheese and I was carrying my pants in my pocket.

The three of us set off nicely relaxed and looking forward to a few jars on the train and a great day out. We got off the train and headed for the town centre. Not entirely sure where the pub was, I stopped a group of lads about 20 years old and asked directions. The conversation started off okay, but he then spotted the Rovers badge embroidered on my shirt. He was a wiry little fucker with a hair-lip and started getting all twitchy.

'You're Bristol!'

'So?'

His mates jumped to attention, but they were really just kids and we were upstanding 40-odd-year-olds, as far as they were concerned.

'Do you know where the pub is or what?'

'Yeah, it's down there.'

'You're fucking Rovers!'

'Congratulations, you can read. Now fuck off.'

Off they trotted, but it was not the last time we saw him and his mates that day.

We found the pub, met the boys and got off to the game. A much quieter time than previous visits to this crap hole.

At the end of the game we were marching in escort to the station and we realised that we were going to be standing on the opposite platform to all the Gasheads going back to Bristol, so we decided to pop back into town for another drink while we waited for our train.

A BRISTOL BOY, PROUD AND BLUE

A quick drink and we headed off towards the station. The station was directly in front, across a road and a small concourse where the wide glass entrance tunnel took you under the tracks to the desired platform. Either side on the corners there was a pub to our right and some sort of office building on the side of the road we were walking.

A few yards before the corner, we needed to cross the road. Around the corner and into view came a group of young lads, late teens or early twenties, walking towards us. At the front was our hair-lipped tour guide we had spoken to earlier that day.

He recognised us and as we walked past I felt a grab on the back of my coat. Taken by surprise, I fell backwards, and as I was falling I looked across and saw Clive land a sweet hook in the jaw of one of them. A familiar smile spread across my face, but not for long, as I was then descended on by a swarm of bees, the kicks started raining in and I covered up as best I could. I felt a stamp on my right hand which broke a bone in my thumb. This was when I said to myself, 'Fuck this, I'm getting up.'

The kicking continued as I climbed to my feet and I swung a wide left arm and caught one of them nicely around the neck, moving him swiftly away from me. Another punch with my right limply got another, but the continued combinations made enough room for me to get away towards the imagined safety of the station. Crossing the road, I saw Adam against the wall with another four or five of them pounding away. I ran over and grabbed the big lad in the middle, yanked his flabby head back and delivered a sweet left to his throat (this was a preferred target during my boxing matches at Beachley, as I was always punching up at the taller boys and it proved more than effective as they would often reel away, choking and gasping for air).

I thought that would help Adam out, but it was much later on the train when he said, 'Thanks for that, but I was holding on to him as protection.'

We made it into the tunnel and thought we would be okay then. Wrong! These boys kept on coming. We continued to walk, though, and stopped to face them every few paces. At least 15 lads and the three of us. I've had worse odds many times before, but I was much younger back then.

We climbed the steps towards the platform and it dawned on me that the last thing I wanted to be doing was scrapping on a railway platform. Only one winner in man versus train.

At the top of the steps there was a left and right option for platforms, with automatic sliding glass doors. Without a word, we turned and stood our ground. My right hand was throbbing and I also had several long scratches on the right side of my face. A little trickle of blood was seeping into my mouth.

As the confrontation wore on, I started to enjoy myself more and more; I felt young again, even if I did say to myself that:

'I shouldn't be here; I'm a grandfather, for fuck's sake!'

Up the steps they raced, and we kept fighting them off. There was one constantly at the front who must have been the village idiot or something – you know, the daft fucker that all his other mates take the piss out of and get him to do the stupid stuff they won't. His face was a bloody mess as every time he got near, one or other of us would slam him back down the steps. I couldn't see this ending, but amazingly we were more than holding our own. We had the higher ground and kept swinging for all we were worth. It was a good old-fashioned punch-up, and I was revelling in it. After yet another charge, we beat them back again and they were then lower down the steps and starting to look a bit unsure of themselves. One of them started waving a mobile phone in the air... 'We got your phone,' he crowed.

We searched our pockets and I realised it was mine, so stupidly I was about to go after it and took a couple of steps back down, when several armour-clad bobbies appeared from the platform and raced by me in pursuit of the Swindon youth.

A train arrived and we all jumped on. Battered, but totally elated. My thumb was swelling up by the second and the side of my face was still dripping. We had to change trains at Reading and thought it sensible to split up to walk through the station, and sure enough the place was crawling with Old Bill.

I received some disapproving looks from Joe Public, so kept my head down and made it to our connection.

During my time at this pub, as well as being able to travel to more games and engaging in all sorts of charity events, I was also able to get a group of us to come up to Bristol for other events.

The most memorable was to see Bad Manners play in the Fleece and Firkin. Five of us travelled from Hampshire and I had arranged to meet some Kingswood lads in the pub next door. With us that night were Alan, who had travelled to Rovers games with me before, accompanied by others not familiar with the unique brand of humour Bristolians can offer. Steve, the provider of the signed shirt, a great friend I had known since the age of 14 through doing a Saturday morning job cleaning out the bakery where my Dad worked, and as funny a guy as you could wish to meet, greeted my companions by individually asking which football team they supported. Bearing in mind there was only one correct answer in his company!!

'Which football team do you follow?' was the question firstly to Alan.

Alan replied, 'Well, you've seen me at Rovers,' and Steve nodded in acknowledgement.

The next guy answered Arsenal. ARSENAL! Steve mused over the answer for a minute and then said, 'Yes. I think I've heard of them'...

He then asked Barry, a very big guy who, of course, Steve had never met, and he replied, 'I don't really like football.'

Fast as you like, Steve replied immediately with, 'Don't like football! You must be gay then.' All in jest, of course, but my fellow travellers didn't know how to take it at all.

Before we went next door for the gig, the advice given by Neil, another Kingswood Rovers fan, was: 'There are Shitheads in here. If it kicks off, raise your arm and we will all steam in!!' I just thought, if it goes off, the last thing I'm going to do is raise an arm that should be swinging.

As we got through security, I had a quick word with Alan, who stood over 6ft 3in, to say, 'Don't start anything in here because the security' – who, by the way, were the biggest group of Hell's Angels I had ever seen, making Alan look like a schoolboy – 'will not just throw you out; they will beat you to a pulp!'

It didn't stop him staggering out of the dancefloor melee with a firm grip on the throat of someone who had upset him. We broke that up and took him outside to cool off. There were a few minor scuffles that night, but it didn't escalate under the watchful eye of the hairy leather-clad bouncers.

TIME TO TALK

My partner at the time was actually working in Bristol and she would always pick up the *Evening Post* for me on Mondays for me to read the match reports. The Monday edition following the fracas at Swindon made for more sobering reading. As I turned the front page, there was a picture of Adam, Clive and myself walking through the station tunnel with the headline **CAN YOU NAME THESE FANS?** The article went on to say that British Transport Police were investigating an incident at Swindon Railway Station and to call their number if you had any information.

By the Monday I had already been to hospital and had my broken hand plastered. The cuts to my face were already healing, but I waited a day or two before I made the call.

'Good morning, British Transport Police, how can I help?'

'Good morning. I'm calling in regard to the appeal in Monday's Bristol *Evening Post*.'

I gave a brief account of the event, saying I was one of the men in the picture and that we were attacked by a large group, broken thumb, lost phone, defended ourselves, and so on.

'Thank you for taking the time to call. I have made a record of all that you have said. Can I just take your name and address, please?'

'I'd rather not give you my name, if you don't mind; my job position is quite sensitive and I would not like to attract attention.'

'Okay then, thank you for your help.'

Two days later I received a call.

'Good morning, sir, is that Mr Slocombe?'

'Yes, it is.'

'This is British Transport Police. I'd like to thank you for your call and would like to invite you to come to Farnborough Police Station to have a little chat. Oh, and bring your mates with you.'

Bollocks, what a dick, not withholding my number.

A day or two later, Adam and I arrived at Farnborough and were greeted by two friendly transport coppers from Bristol.

'Where's the other one?' they asked.

Adam replied that he was working away and couldn't make it. Which was partly true. We were both cautioned and taken to individual rooms to be interviewed.

I was asked to talk through the whole story and I got the impression that we were genuinely there to help with the investigation and not about to be charged. Why should we, when we had honestly done no more than defend ourselves? Adam was undergoing the same experience, and around an hour later we were all together in one room.

'Did you hit anyone?' I was asked directly.

'Well, if I did, it was purely in self-defence.'

'Well, you defended yourselves quite well; as a group, they suffered a broken jaw, collar bone and several lost teeth.'

It was hard trying to hide my delight.

Then they produced a huge photo album and in it were at least 40 CCTV photographs, starting at the entrance to the station, into the tunnel and up onto the landing at the top of the stairs.

There we all were, in glorious grainy colour. For identification purposes we had all been labelled with a little round orange sticker. The three of us were 1, 2 and 3. The numbers continued on to 16; there were a few others there, but not close enough to the action to warrant a number.

The officers explained after we had given our stories that this particular group of lads had been terrorising the Thames Valley, causing trouble in Oxford and at home for a little while.

As we looked through the pictures, it became apparent that this altercation must have lasted a little while. The photos all had times on them, and the coppers said that it had gone on for around 20 minutes. It seemed the pictures were selected to ensure we were not over-incriminated, as not one showed any of us actually throwing a punch or kick. In fact, they were quite comical to look at, because while it was going on I would have sworn that the three of us were stood shoulder to shoulder like the Thin Blue Line. In reality, there were times when Clive had stepped through the door onto the platform, and one where I appeared to stand back, almost like I was having a tea break. Clive at one point was holding our coats, and I hadn't even remembered taking it off. Then in the next, Adam and I would be stuck fully in the middle of several of them at the top of the stairs. You could see the mess on the Village Idiot's face and pictures of guys toppling backwards down the stairs, as if pushed by some unseen entity.

Our friendly lawmen thanked us and asked if we could get Clive to call and that they would be happy to interview him at his home. I suggested that they could come to my pub to talk to him and we could stage a re-enactment for them.

Later, we talked to Clive and wound him up for a few hours, saying that we were all getting charged with GBH and affray and the pictures were really incriminating, especially that right hook he landed across the street. He was crapping himself for ages until we told him the truth.

The Police eventually charged six of the gang, two of whom were brothers from a quite wealthy family – obviously spoilt brats. Those two and one other received short prison sentences.

At my pub every New Year's Eve we would hold a big compulsory fancy dress party, with ticket-only admission for around 180 customers. We would have a different theme each year, ranging from Arabian Nights to Titanic, and the theme we chose for the night following this was Wild West. Adam, Clive and myself dressed as the Three Amigos, with orange cardboard discs glued to our sombreros numbered 1, 2 and 3.

The first New Year we were there, the theme was TV characters. The first year, and every subsequent one, always astounded me by the inventiveness of the customers. This first year, a group of customers came as the cast of *Toy Story*: Woody, Bo Peep and Mr Potato Head. I really felt for the green Marine swathed in polythene – he reckoned he lost around 7lb in weight that evening. With all tickets sold and the evening going well, I had a shout from the person taking the admissions at the door. A couple of blokes had turned up with their wives, demanding to be let in.

'I'm very sorry, sir, but it's ticket-only admission tonight and compulsory fancy dress.'

'You can't refuse me entry, it's a public house.'

'Again, I will say that this is a private party; but for your information, I can refuse you entry for whatever reason I deem fit.'

'That's bollocks. I'm coming in.'

I then said to him, **'Look, do you really want to go to work on Monday and tell all your colleagues that Andy Pandy kicked you out of the pub tonight?!!'**

He looked at me dressed in a lovely blue striped smock and bonnet, my rosy red cheeks not offering a glimpse of a smile, and decided he wasn't going to get anywhere and walked off down the path and into the night, thoroughly dejected.

NO PLACE FOR THE OLD

If the experience at Swindon taught me anything, it was: however exciting it had been, the violence should be left for the young. We all grow up eventually, and now my time at football should be used actually watching a bit more of it. Rovers were once again not setting the world alight, and times in the early noughties were a much quieter affair. As I had been away from Bristol for some years, it became a pleasure when I could get down to pick up my Dad and take him to the football, along with Adam, Clive and my brother.

As far as Dad was concerned, anyone from west of Swindon was a Londoner, and he was quick to say so. During the usual row over who was buying the first round, Adam or Clive would get the money out and ask, 'What you drinking, Ivor?'

Dad would say, 'No, no, I'll get 'em. Look, I know how dear your houses are up London, mind, and you come down 'ere, all you ever got is £20 notes. I'll get 'em in.' Every week the same and always entertaining. He was a wonderfully funny man, and 14 years on we still miss him. We would vary the pubs that we drank in, with him favouring the Vic or Wellington. The two pubs were like chalk and cheese; the Vic a smaller, bustling and busy pub on match days and the Wellington a much larger establishment which stood in a commanding position at the top of Muller Road next to the common. It had a large beer garden to the left and rear, with parking also on the left as you look at the pub in front of the garden. In front of the pub, that stands on a junction of three roads, is a wide tarmac and cobble parking area; this is given over to drinking customers on match days and is a good place to stand and survey the delights of Horfield, with views across our side of Bristol. The Memorial Stadium is situated across the other side of the busy Gloucester Road and straight ahead down one of a few side streets, no more than 400 yards.

At one game, we were at the bar in the Duke of Wellington and there were a few away fans further around the bar. The noise got louder and a small scuffle started, so straight away Dad took his glasses off and stuck them in his pocket. 'Calm down, Ivor,' said Adam. I'm sure if he'd been born around the time we were, he may have behaved exactly like us.

During his final months, he was under the care of the Macmillan Nurses, and during a conversation his love of Rovers was mentioned.

'Do you know, he once drove eleven and a half hours to watch them in Newcastle? No motorways then, mind' and **'He queued all the way to Ashley Road for tickets.'**

Bristol Rovers are very active in the community, and Dad was invited as a guest of the club, along with my brother and I, to the last game of the season. We met the stadium representative in the Blackthorn End bar and were told that we had seats in a box, with lunch being served. Also that anything at all that we wanted that day was courtesy of the club. Dad was extremely poorly by this time, but he started his pint of Guinness and held on to it for all he was worth. From the bar, we had to walk to the West Stand where the executive boxes were, and in order to we needed to pass through a security gate. The jobsworth attendant spotted that Dad was still clinging onto his sole pint and said, 'You can't bring that through here.'

My brother, who was known for having a short fuse, stepped forward, bristling with anger. I jumped in front and explained the situation, quietly finishing with, 'Don't you fucking dare try to take that drink off him!!!'

He apologised and we were let through and found our way upstairs. Dad met the Manager and some other officials, before we took our seats. A wonderful padded seat with a great view, close to the noise of the Blackthorn End. We could see Dad soaking up the atmosphere, and he turned and looked at us through glazed eyes.

'This is all right, kid,' he said. This once fit man, nine and a half stone dripping wet but quick and strong, was just a shadow of his former self, and we wanted to make a lasting memory for us all.

'Yes, Dad. Look, you couldn't stretch this out for a couple of years, could you?'

'I'll do my best, kid, I'll do my best,' he said.

Rovers won. We assured him we would look after Mum, as that had been one of his first questions, and he looked as contented as we had ever seen him. He passed away just a few weeks later, with us all at his bedside. The strength he displayed in his final days was immense. Never a complaint about the pain he must have endured. *Goodnight Irene* and *Abide With Me* were played at his funeral, as for many years Dad had always managed to get a ticket for the FA Cup Final. Blue and white wreaths and flowers were in abundance. It was a mark of his standing that several friends of both my brother and I attended the funeral.

After Dad had passed away, I found it really hard to attend a game at all. I missed the following season and sort of got out of the habit, always, though, looking for the scores and agonising over the lack of progress. Eventually, I decided I would take my football-mad grandson to a game. He was around six or seven and also living in Hampshire, as my daughter moved there soon after he was born. I always knew from the moment he was born, four days before I hit 40, that the first real football match he went to would be a Rovers game, and I, of course, would take him. I was surprised that I wasn't reported for child cruelty. As he was still quite young, I got tickets in the East Stand front row. He absolutely adored it, watching every kick and soaking up the experience. Later, when he was older and able to sit in the pub, I took him to a game at Brentford. Standing on the terrace, this for him was an even better experience, stepping down in front of me, enthralled by not only the game but the chanting coming from the hundreds of Gasheads present. In hindsight, I think he helped my grieving process.

Now, although he has a love for the Premiership and Arsenal in particular, he is always ready to come to watch the Gas, his first team, with me, and my signed and framed shirt is displayed proudly on his bedroom wall.

A DOWNWARD SPIRAL

The seasons came and went, and mid-table or worse was the best we could achieve. My appearances were few and far between because I had left the pub business and was now working in the mainstream, without stress but having to work one in three weekends, Saturday and Sunday. Invariably, the weeks I wasn't working they were playing way up north, and this was the week set aside to visit Mum. Or they were home and I was working. It wasn't as though I was missing much on the pitch, but you also start to lose touch with where everybody is drinking before the game and wondering if they were all standing in another part of the ground. You feel a little bit like an outsider.

In 2011, we suffered relegation again to what was now League Two – Fourth Division in old money, and very worrying. The slide continued, with the team struggling through to finish mid-table again for the next two seasons, before the unthinkable happened. Relegation to the Conference in 2014. In all honesty, the writing had been on the wall, and it was with a sense of resignation when it finally happened.

Before this, Dave and I had decided to hold a party for Mum's 80th birthday. Mum quickly got involved in the organisation, insisting that all the grandchildren would receive a gift from her and we should do this for everybody and that for others. As always, Mum was considerate and wanted everyone to have a good time. She had never had any sort of party in her honour before, and she seemed almost embarrassed to be the centre of attention. I called in on my regular visit a few weeks before and noticed she had bought a new block of laser-sharp knives to 'cut the cake' with.

'Blimey, Mum, these will cut steel! Why did you get them?'

'I don't want to use any old knife. I wants a proper 'un for the cake.'

Shopping was one of Mum's favourite pastimes; she was amazing with their limited funds, but always so smartly dressed. Her favourite lines when she would say she had been shopping would be, 'I'll show you', and she would walk to her bedroom and retrieve the latest purchase. Then, ten minutes later, a repeat, 'I'll show you', and the next in the fashion parade would be collected from the wardrobe that must have had the capacity of Narnia.

When my Dad was alive, he would often comment, 'Is that new, Louise?'

'No, Ivor, I've had it ages.' Not even attempting to hide the tag still attached to whatever blouse or pair of trousers she was displaying.

At the party, everyone gathered to honour our head of the family, as Mum was now the eldest of all her surviving siblings. A short speech by Mum just asking everyone to enjoy themselves and thanking them for coming, and the cake was cut. Mum then took a seat, and all the grandkids were called up to collect their goodie bags. Meanwhile, an aunt decided she was the most qualified to portion the cake, and promptly sliced through several fingers and an emergency run to nearby Frenchay Hospital was called for.

At this time, I had not lived in Bristol for nearly 25 years, and for the most part it had been a good move. There were times, however, when I missed being closer to home. The following March proved to be the most that I had regretted being so far away. I had been out of the pub business for over five years and found myself less stressed just employed driving large vehicles doing home deliveries. I was on a delivery in Epsom when I received a call from Dave. I knew it was bad news, because he hardly ever called. My fears were well founded with two words. 'It's Mum.'

I felt sick and my legs buckled as Dave continued to tell me that Mum had been found on the floor and it looked like she had suffered a stroke. This was really bad news for Mum because she had suffered strokes twice before, the first in her 40s, which, remarkably, she had made a complete recovery from. But this was different. Mum was much older and I just knew in my heart that it would be terminal. I got the rest of my load taken off by a support van, and then drove the 50-odd miles or so back to base. With a maximum speed of 56 miles an hour, it seemed to take an eternity. The drive from my home to Bristol, another 80-odd miles, not surprisingly took less time. We sat at Mum's hospital bedside for three days before she passed away. It had been nine years since we lost Dad, and Mum had missed him every day. In the months prior to her passing, she did odd things, like having all the birthday cards written for the whole year. She also started giving items of jewellery away for no apparent reason. I believe Mum knew her time was close and secretly looked forward to being reunited with Dad.

On an earlier visit to the cemetery, Mum commented that the stone had sunk and I said I would get it fixed. She said, 'Make sure you get it done before I'm in there; I hate low ceilings.'

Mum was every bit as funny as Dad at times.

At the funeral, it fell on me to deliver the eulogy. Having spent so many years in the pub industry, public speaking was normally an easy task. This, however, was more difficult than I imagined, but I hope I managed to present the speech well enough. In the car after the ceremony, one of my elderly uncles commented that I had done a good job and that they wouldn't be able to stand up and speak like that. I just looked at all three of Mum's brothers and said, '**Well, I am available for bookings.**' My uncles and Dave all laughed, relieving the sadness we all felt at the time.

At the interment, I took Mum's ashes and placed them next to Dad. It was the last thing I could do for them both.

BETTER TIMES TO COME

The threat of relegation had hung heavy over the club all season, despite not occupying a relegation spot until the very last game of the season, a depressing loss at home to Mansfield Town. Earlier in the year, the first Bristol Derby had taken place since 2007 at Ashton Gate. Normal service had been resumed between the two sets of fans, with around 40 arrests. We took the summer off and prepared for the unknown. It was going to prove to be a time of resurgence at last. A new manager with little league experience had come in too late to prevent the drop, but Darrell Clarke would achieve legendary status for his honest and passionate approach to management.

In a strange way, the forthcoming foray strengthened the bond with the club. We had all witnessed the years of struggle and maybe we needed to hit rock bottom to start the climb back. Although languishing in the very depths of the football pyramid, we were about to enjoy a calendar of fixtures for the first time since the glory days at Twerton Park.

We returned for the following August favourites to be promoted, but history had shown the road back can be tricky, to say the least. The Conference in reality was by now a bona fide fifth division, boasting full-time teams, many of whom had held the coveted status of League clubs just like us. A glance at the map was required to locate some of the places we were going to play. Braintree was high on my list because of my friends there, and Woking and Eastleigh were easily accessible for me. At one of the games during the season, I bumped into Jay, our souvenir seller, and said that in all honesty I was quite enjoying the season. He agreed, but said, 'As long as it's just the one year, though.'

After a poor start we were making great strides, and once again the Gasheads were following in numbers the Conference had probably never seen. We were constantly outnumbering the home crowds. Woking away, and my brother came to me and we took the train along with my grandson; great, a real drink and a laugh with the boys. Woking Football Club were confident that no tickets were necessary for the away fans, really not taking any note of our following. They had capacity for just shy of 2000 away fans; we got in, but some 300 were locked outside. Many years ago, at an FA Cup tie against Fulham, thousands of Rovers fans turned up with forged tickets that were promptly being destroyed by the Police. Of course, everyone protested that theirs was a valid ticket and your dopey plod have ripped it up. Fearing a full-scale riot, the gates were opened and we all poured in. At Woking, the unfortunates left outside mainly just decided to go back to the pubs.

The unfamiliar destinations kept coming: Nuneaton, Alfreton and Welling were never on our road map, and even the likes of Wrexham and Halifax, ex-League teams who had found it hard to extricate themselves from the grip of the Conference, were now on our destination to visit. We needed to put many of these teams away if we were not to suffer the same fate. The excitement was building as we progressed deeper and deeper into the season. After a worryingly slow start, the momentum and feel-good feeling was back. All well and good, but in the early part of the season it seemed the games I managed to get to we either lost or played out a draw. Braintree was an example of that. After defeat to Forest Green in October, Rovers then went 20 games before suffering their next loss. The dip in form was temporary, as we finished the last eight games undefeated, culminating in a 7-0 thrashing of Alfreton Town on the last day of the regular season, condemning them to relegation. The 7-0 scoreline equalled our biggest league win margin for some 51 years.

Rovers were, however, pipped to the post for automatic promotion by one point by Barnet. So it was to be the play-offs and a possible trip to Wembley. Here come the nerves again. The semi-final, played over two legs, was against Forest Green, to whom we had suffered one of only five defeats during the season. Away leg first, and Rovers came away with a crucial 1-0 win. I took my future wife/former employee Wendy to the game and stood on the Blackthorn End in a record attendance at any regular season game in the Conference. The Memorial Stadium isn't that big, with limited capacity, and a new stadium is desperately needed to achieve any real success. But on that early May day, with the sun shining, the 11,000 that were there created an atmosphere in my mind to match any ground.

With the slender lead from the first game, confidence and yet nerves were constant companions. That was until the 24th minute, when Chris Lines, a Bristolian by birth, scored to make it 2-0 on aggregate. The whole ground erupted with utter joy. The Blackthorn End was a mass of leaping bodies, and Wendy disappeared in the throng. In an instant she had been carried away in the euphoric celebrations. We managed to find each other when the crowd settled down. *Goodnight Irene* rang out loudly and for longer than normal, and as we approached half-time, the nerves receded and we could all genuinely enjoy the game and start thinking about our next visit to the national stadium.

As the second half progressed, Rovers were by now in complete control, and I said to Wendy, 'Be prepared, we're going to score again soon,' such was the manner of play. Sure enough, Matty Taylor netted in the 88th minute to put the tie well and truly to bed. We managed to stay together during the prolonged celebrations.

Two long weeks later, and North Bristol took the pilgrimage to North-West London. My journey was shorter and the day out became a family affair, with my son Lewis and his boy, the middle of my three grandsons, my eldest grandson and Wendy taking the train to Waterloo and riding the tube. My grandsons were resplendent in suitable blue and white attire. We arranged to meet up with my brother and one of his boys at a pub on Baker Street. That didn't go well; as we arrived, the security weren't letting any more people in, and across the road a meeting of Young Gasheads and our opponent's fans had escalated into a large brawl. As I was on a family day out, I had to resist the primeval urge to get involved. I managed to have a word with my brother Dave and collected our tickets from him, saying we would meet later outside the ground.

Walking down Wembley Way, the scene was so familiar and there always seemed to be a carnival feeling. The multitude of food and beverage vendors were charging extortionate prices for average products, but who cared? We were there for a party and to get us back where we belonged. There were scores of souvenir sellers, but for once Jay was taking a day off. Ticket touts, with their shifty demeanour, were buying and selling with their chins tucked low to avoid the prying eyes of the big brother cameras. We arrived around two hours before the game and there was already a sea of Blue, White and Black – the quarters we wear and the stripes of Grimsby Town, who were back at Wembley for the third time seeking to at last win and get promoted at our expense.

As we got closer to the huge national stadium, the colour palate changed as the two sets of fans tried to decipher which way around the vast arena to go in order to find the right numbered gate. Stripes went mainly left and we gravitated to the right. Two huge bar areas were set up in the shadow of the stadium, one primarily for us, the other, of course, for the Grimsby crowd. We got some drinks in floppy plastic glasses and waited for the other members of our clan to arrive. Amongst the thousands of fans in this huge area, we found ourselves having a drink three yards from a cousin of ours and his boy. When we were all together, we managed a really nice memorable photo of us all.

We filed into the stadium and nervously waited for the game to get underway. Once again we outnumbered the opposition by many thousands, but they cheered their team on with equal fervour.

With only two minutes of the game gone, Grimsby scored, causing huge celebrations far away at the other end of the ground. We were silent for a minute or two, but regained our voices to rally our team. Mid-way through the first half, to our utter delight, Ellis Harrison equalised. The game was only 30 minutes in and we had been through the mill with our emotions, from despair to joy.

All square at half-time and much-needed refreshment was taken on board. There was a loud humming in the concourse as hordes of nervous supporters discussed the last 45 minutes and the next.

The second half was just a nervy blur as both teams were wary of making any sort of mistake, and predictably at the whistle the teams remained locked at 1-1. Extra time, and then the most edge-of-your-seat event in football: penalties. Extra time flew by in an instant and we were at the scenario which if you win it's the best feeling imaginable, but the worst if you lose.

Unusually, our Manager substituted the goalkeeper before the start of the penalties, bringing on Steve Mildenhall, who was much taller than Will Puddy, the man he replaced. At the time, although an unusual move, it made perfect sense to me and made me feel a little more confident. Rovers were to take the first penalty, and Bristol's own Chris Lines stepped up and scored. Craig Disley, a former Rovers player, levelled it up for Grimsby. The next two penalties were also scored, and Lee Brown stepped up for our third. Another went in, 3-2. The pressure on the players was building and it showed, as the next Grimsby player, Pittman, blasted his penalty over the bar, to the delight of the 30,000 at the other end of Wembley. The Grimsby fans buried their heads in their hands and it was made worse for them as Rovers scored the fourth. Clay stepped up for Grimsby, needing to score to keep them in. He slotted it away well and our final penalty fell to Lee Mansell. If he scored he would make himself a hero for eternity among the Gas; fail and it was possibly sudden death. Penalties, I mean, not for him.

Darrell Clarke, the Manager, unable to keep still for a moment, was jumping nervously in a line of coaches and players, all with their arms interlocked behind their backs. The Grimsby faithful were making as much noise as possible to try and distract our player as he ran up and scored. We, of course, all went absolutely crazy, grown men crying and hugging complete strangers. As all the players rushed away to the other end to engulf our new hero Lee Mansell, the Manager raced in the opposite direction towards the jubilant Rovers fans. We celebrated in the ground for an age before the team composed itself and climbed the famous steps to receive a trophy in recognition of an unforgettable season. The first team to bounce straight back up after relegation to the Conference in 10 years. A feat last achieved by Carlisle United in 2005.

Rovers were back, and our rollercoaster ride was back on the rise. The following season was to bring much, much more, both on and off the pitch.

IT'S ALL COMING TOGETHER

Wendy and I were now engaged and planning our wedding. We were also about to buy a house which was going to occupy me for the next four years, as it needed a complete refurbishment. It had been home to an elderly lady who had lived there since it was built in 1975. They had decorated the house in 1976 and left it at that. Wendy had viewed it first and could see a vision; all I could see was an awful lot of work. It was detached, with four bedrooms and two bathrooms and a downstairs WC, all different colours of the rainbow. There were questionable stains on the carpets that seemed to be welded to the floor and a gas fire typical of its age, with hammered copper facing and a large wooden surround. Every time I got around to ripping out one or other of these articles, someone would invariably say, 'You could get good money for that' or 'Turquoise baths are very in now; you could sell that or keep it.'

When I always replied with, **'Do you want it?'**, the standard answer would be, 'Oh, no, I don't want it!'

With everything going on, getting out to a game was a great break from whatever DIY chore I was currently undertaking.

The first thoughts for most fans after a promotion, and particularly for us just arriving back into the Football League, must be consolidation. Don't get relegated, stay in the division. Mid-table will be fine.

Rovers, like so many seasons before, had started with a loss and relatively indifferent form, but soon hit their stride, climbing the table and performing well home and away. Trips to Portsmouth, again an easy one for me, were good – not for that particular result, but to see the same old faces again and again on the road, all looking a little older, but crucially still possessing the same sort of humour. It felt good again; so good that, for my stag day/night, I decided to book a box at the Memorial Stadium for the last game of the season versus Dagenham and Redbridge. Little did I know at the time what an inspired choice it was to be.

We would have to wait for a few months before that, and a wedding shortly after and a honeymoon to Mexico; it really was all coming together.

We started the mammoth task of bringing our home kicking and screaming into the 21st century. The major building works first, and an extension to make way for a new large kitchen. During these works we bought the cheapest electric cooker we could and wired it in with enough cable for it to be in a different position every day, according to the builders' requirements. Wendy performed miracles in the forest of Acrow props supporting the rear of the building. Every bit of the house was tackled from the top by replacing all the soffits down to the ground and buying new drain covers. Not one part of the fabric of the house was neglected. I felt that for every completed job I should get to a game. Not that many games in a season, though.

IT'S ALL COMING TOGETHER

The planning for our wedding was picking up pace. It was to be a second marriage for both of us, and although, as is traditional, you pay for it yourself, we still wanted to have a special day, inviting our closest family and friends to all stay at a local hotel where the wedding was to be held.

Rovers were staying with the pace, and optimism was building. New owners had purchased the club and promises were made. Investment at last – we really were on the up. The Al Qadis, a Jordanian banking family and quite wealthy, had invested in our club, and Wael Al Qadi in particular was a real football fan, following Chelsea during his time living in London. Towards the end of the season we were again in promotion form. Prior to the last game, we had won 10, drawn 2 and lost only 1 game. A win at home could see us promoted again if results fell right.

I drew up my invite list for my Stag number 1. Stag 2 was back home where I lived, and the guys in our social circle were treating me to a day out karting and the obligatory Indian, with lashings of beer. I had a great time with them, but the excitement of the impending game could not be beaten. The Executive Box for the final game. Fifteen bodies needed, and getting the list down was tough. But the honoured party consisted of my son Lewis, brother Dave and his Gashead son Scott (not his eldest, who, although a thoroughly nice young man, was a City fan). When he started going over to the other side, I did remember asking Dave if he was very disappointed. The list continued, and Nigel the hippy drummer, who by now was living near Glasgow and flew down for the day, made the cut. Three guys whom Wendy and I had met on our first holiday were Martin from Braintree, another lad, Steve from Ipswich, and Frankie, a bonny chatty Scotsman who was living in Wiltshire and a diehard Rangers fan. Their wives also came and spent the day out and about, enjoying the sights of Bristol with Wendy. The rest of our esteemed group were my closest Kingswood Gasheads and another old friend Brian, who had arranged my first ever mortgage, and Ken the drunken cyclist.

For the people that had travelled, we had arranged a hotel in central Bristol in readiness for the two groups to meet up in the evening for a table of 25 or so booked into a nice Spanish restaurant.

Meeting at the hotel, a minibus was booked to get us to the Wellington Arms for pre-drinking drinks. The girls had planned a trip on an open-top bus with stops at most alcohol-selling establishments, to include the Avon Gorge Hotel; very nice, but no competition for the day I had planned.

We boarded the bus and started our journey across the centre, and foolishly the cab driver took us onto Stokes Croft and up the Gloucester Road; sure the most direct route, but this was the main A38 road leading out of Bristol, with traffic from all directions crossing it or joining it. There was row after row of shops, all individual in the merchandise they sold, and restaurants of every type. After Stokes Croft, we passed through St Andrews and the edge of Redland, both student accommodation meccas, so subsequently also home to several Vegan eating houses; luckily you can still get an Indian or kebab – it's not totally lost to the vegetarian eco-warriors. Bristolians will know that traffic-wise this was not a good idea. We started our painful crawl up towards Horfield and the Memorial Stadium, with a raging thirst starting and passing pub after pub. Shortly before the prison, with about a mile to go we bailed out and said we would walk, making arrangements to be picked up around 6pm.

As much as we would have liked, we couldn't stop for a drink in any of the pubs between alighting from the taxi, as we were meeting the rest of our party in the Wellington Arms.

The route march started, and very quickly Brian fell off the pace. We waited and let him catch up.

'You buggers are going to give me a heart attack,' he gasped. Brian was a few years older than me, and years of sitting at a desk, with a healthy appetite combined with business lunches, had taken its toll.

'Go on, I'll get there soon enough; just get me a nice Malt Whisky, so I've got something to look forward to.'

We didn't argue with him and raced ahead, still managing to get in and secure some tables near the bar before it got too busy. The large area at the front of the pub was already packed with expectant fans, daring to dream. The ciders were flowing and the other guys all arrived around the same time as a wheezing Brian. The first two or three of Scotland's finest barely touched the sides and his recovery was complete. A good hour and a half of good-humoured drinking before we had to walk the three or four hundred yards to the ground. Mercifully for Brian, it was downhill now.

Shown to our box and introduced to the ladies who would be serving us, we set about ordering drinks and finding our seats. We were in the last but one box away from the noisy Blackthorn End and vociferous home support.

Steve, the supplier of the signed shirt many years earlier, and one of the Kingswood lads that I had personally known since we were 14 and doing a Saturday job in a bakery where my Dad worked, arrived late and promptly presented me with another shirt, this time a Black Club and Country Polo Shirt. What a nice thing to do, and it went on immediately. In the box next to us were another few guys we knew, also mainly from Kingswood – it was turning into some party.

The build-up to the game continued and we had a visit from Ellis Harrison and a couple of other players. Photos were taken and we settled down for a tense first half. We started the day in fourth place with Accrington in third. We needed to better the result of our closest rivals for automatic promotion, and only twelve minutes in it looked like it wasn't going to be our day. Dagenham and Redbridge scored and a huge dejected slump was felt. So, typically for us who had lived through this torment before, we ordered another round of drinks.

Before they had arrived, Billy Bodin had equalised and it was game-on again. Somebody else ordered another round to celebrate. I was starting to think I had better slow down or I'd miss the Tapas later.

But it was no day for taking it easy. The drinks continued to flow, and Brian entered a whisky drinking competition with Scottish Frankie. He was confident of victory, but it was not going to be Bannockburn today. Brian, a seasoned and accomplished drinker, left Frankie a slurring shadow of the confident former soldier.

Half-time, and the teams were locked together at one each. Accrington, also playing at home, were currently scoreless.

During the interval, a hot buffet was served and the new Chairman, Wael Al Qadi, made his rounds, introducing himself and pleasantly talking to many fans. We got to talk for a minute or two and the

IT'S ALL COMING TOGETHER

customary selfies were taken. Dave and myself, in a quiet moment, both mentioned how much Dad would have enjoyed the day, and we raised our glasses to him.

The second half started, and throughout the game Rovers were dominant with 35 attempts at goal, but failing to get the vital breakthrough.

Accrington Stanley were playing Stevenage and it remained a blank scoreline. We were approaching full-time and the tension was rising. How could Rovers not have scored? Shot after shot were repelled by the Dagenham defence and goalkeeper. The board went up to indicate how many minutes were going to be added and it showed five. A deep rising roar resonated around the whole stadium. Still nil-nil up north! Come on Rovers! For the umpteenth time that day, a loud chorus of *Goodnight Irene* engulfed the Memorial Stadium, and two minutes into added time Lee Brown from the middle of the Dagenham area shoots and scores the goal that sent the whole ground and our box ecstatic. For the second time within a year, the pure unadulterated joy flowed from us all. The crescendo of noise seemed to be much louder than the 11,000 present should have been able to generate. The celebrations for the goal went on and on. The scorer was booked for his part in the extended celebration.

The game restarted and the longest three minutes ever began to unfold. Dagenham were beaten, and all ears were waiting for news from the Lancashire town. The final whistle blew and the unstoppable pitch invasion ensued. Thousands made it on to the pitch and our bird's eye view of the carnival was amazing. However, the massed gathering was still waiting for confirmation. The blue touch paper could not be lit and the corks remained unpopped until, after an agonising wait, the news we all wanted to hear started to filter around. Pockets of cheering grew and grew until once again the Memorial Stadium erupted in a thunderous roar. I for one ranted like a demented soul at the news and realisation that after years of turmoil we had indeed returned. The fans sang 'We've got our Rovers back' and the emotions rose in the eyes of the long-suffering Gasheads.

Steve from Ipswich was not a football fan at all, but seeing the utter joy on our faces, he promptly ordered seven bottles of champagne and we quaffed them down, and another order went in. The scenes on the pitch where the thousands of jubilant Gasheads were milling around is engraved on my memory. We happily hung around as we had to wait for the taxi, but as the throng moved away the new owner was located and Wael Al Qadi was carried shoulder-high out of the ground and down Gloucester Road to the Queen Vic pub. The Queen Vic was a small boozer around 500 yards from the Rovers ground, sat next to a garage and opposite several fast food outlets. It had become very popular in recent years with a slightly older football crowd, leaving the livelier John Cabot (The Royal Oak, its original name), a little further down the road to the up and coming new band of Gasheads. On a match day, the Queen Vic would get very crowded and inevitably customers would spill out onto the road. That evening, though, the whole road, a main thoroughfare into the city, was blocked by the crowd. Buses and traffic were at a standstill with no sign of being able to move any time soon as swarms of celebrating fans hugged anyone at all. The drinks flowed long into the night all over North and East Bristol. This time, the taxi driver was smart enough to divert down Muller Road, the long road Rob and I had run down several times as 16-year-old squaddies. Even this road, over an hour and a half after the game, was congested. Car horns were blasting away their congratulations to Bristol's oldest team. We eventually passed the

IT'S ALL COMING TOGETHER

old Eastville Stadium site and made our way up and onto the M32 motorway back towards town. Looking across at the place where I had basically grown up, now with a huge IKEA on the spot the Tote End used to be, I thought at least the Swedish store is painted Blue.

By the time we reached the hotel, my voice had been reduced to a croak. The girls had arrived back from their sunny sightseeing tour. They didn't need to ask how it went as we were all the worse for wear. I, though, was still high as a kite, the adrenaline rushing through me as I absorbed not only the current day, but the events of the last year or so. Francis in particular was having trouble standing, let alone walking. We all needed to shower and get ready for our night out. The restaurant booking was only an hour away and we obviously had to have a pre-dinner aperitif. Our powers of recuperation seemed to work, and within the allocated timescale we were ready to go. We had a drink in the Shakespeare on Princes Street, again a road that held the memory of the meeting on the centre and then the walk of many thousands to Ashton Gate.

Way back then, as we left the centre and entered Princes Street with its tall hotel on the right and behind that the floating harbour, to the left in front of the regal Georgian Queens Square, buildings of a much older period than the hotel. Standing the test of time, their uses long ago homes for the wealthy seafarers, but now offices to an assortment of financial businesses. This corridor of commerce was witness to the chanting and singing from the Blue half of Bristol as the sound echoed and resonated around the high grey walls.

We were eating in the former Port House, now a Spanish Tapas restaurant, and the evening meant to celebrate our forthcoming wedding doubled up as an amazing group of friends just created a few memories that would certainly stay with me forever.

Wendy and I visited the cemetery the next day, before heading back along the M4 and home, placing flowers, which we would do again with Wendy's bouquet after our wedding day. I spoke to both parents, wishing Mum could have been coming to our big day and telling Dad that the box at football was not the same without him. He would have said, 'This is all right, kid, isn't it?'

My daughter Sarah did a wonderful thing for me before the wedding. She had some cufflinks made with a picture of Mum on one and Dad on the other. I wore them with pride.

WHAT DOES IT ALL MEAN?

I hope you have persevered with my ramblings. My wife jokingly said, 'If I had known all this about you years ago, we may not have got married.' I think she was joking – at least I hope so. I offered the reasoning that I am a different person now, but I am not. I am just a different version of the same me. Steve Mark 2.6 or 3.5, however many changes there have been. As I said at the beginning of this story, you need experiences to become experienced. If you have never made a mistake, you have probably never done anything. I have overcome trauma, arrests, marital breakdown, mental illness, redundancy and the odd good kicking. I have also handed out a couple of decent beatings. There have been times when confronted that I have felt that I was going to get a proper battering, but I have always stood my ground. If you are prepared to stand up and be counted, pure front may save you a hiding now and again. All these things have contributed to who I am, so I make no apologies. As I approach later life, retirement and all that may bring, I feel happier than I have ever been, mainly courtesy of my wonderful wife. I am also blessed with two children, both making their way in life, and five grandchildren, all totally different from each other, but each one making me equally proud and excited to see what adults they become. I also have two stepsons that have welcomed me into their mother's life, who again are achieving success in their chosen professions.

Reflecting on my story, I don't think it is very different from many boys born into similar circumstances as me. Large towns and cities all have areas of deprivation; several have football teams, and during those times, trouble at football was rife. I like to think I inherited my humorous side from not only my parents, but also from my home city. The friendships I have made over my life, some approaching 50 years and the ones more recent, are equally important to me. If only we all had more time to see each other regularly. Looking through my life at the time, it becomes apparent that after starting small, learning the craft and taking the lessons – albeit painfully sometimes – the whole story is just one of growing up and following your peers to earn respect. Eventually, you rein in your behaviour, not only because you feel you need to, but also because you realise you want to.

In recent years there have been a few reunions of the Tote End Old Boys, usually held in some pub before and after a home game. To see all the old faces was a treat, knowing that the passion for our club still burns in us. Just being presented with a little Tote End Old Boys badge was like a badge of honour, a belonging if you like. Jay, our entrepreneurial souvenir salesman, has produced a huge flag dedicated to Tote End Old Boys and Girls that have sadly passed away. Looking at the names and recognising so many brings home my own mortality. I have said to my wife and close friends that my only ambition when I go is to have my name embroidered onto that flag. I hope I've done enough to merit a place. I'll stitch it on myself if needed. After all, I have the skill – I learned to do that at 15.

The Coronavirus epidemic and lockdown meant that all football stopped for a while. It dawned on me that I never missed the Premiership on Sky TV at all. But even though I haven't been as frequent a visitor to watch Rovers recently, I really missed them. So

I made a promise that I would get to more games. I could dispose of Sky Sports altogether and spend the money each month on my first true love. The plan is for my wife and I to spend more weekends in Bristol and to make the match days into match weekends with the complete package: hotel, football, a few drinks and good restaurants. I love my home town, and the chance to spend more time here fills me with joy. After all, I am 'A Bristol Boy, Proud and Blue'.

Acknowledgements

When you have to sit down and think about who to thank for the long and personal journey we all travel, the obvious candidates must spring to mind. You would think! I wish to thank the people who inspired me, respected and corrected me when I strayed too close to the wind. Without them my story could have taken a very different track. These are my champions.

Mum and Dad. Wonderful parents, devoted to each other as well as their sons. Hardworking, salt of the Earth, hilariously funny, even during the tough times in the beginning and at the end.

The British Army. That brief time in uniform taught me respect and control. In one fell swoop, it toughened me not only physically but mentally as well. Dealing with drunken dickheads during the pub years was possible due to the discipline drilled into me.

My Heroes of the Tote End. Too many to mention. But **Rod**, we all still miss you.

Tater, Rich, Colin, Steve and all the Easton boys. What a gang of lads to grow up with.

Kevin and Sheila. My wonderful constant friends. **Bridget**, my first wife, taught me that there was much more to reach for. With her, the success in our pub career was a springboard to prove anything is possible.

Brian and Jacqui. Always a bed for the night, when needed. Stilton and Port, mainly Port.

The remarkable **surgeons and staff of the NHS.** My appalling accident-prone nature gave them all so much work.

Sarah and Lewis, my children. They always forgave me my shortcomings and then gave me five wonderful grandchildren. Sarah is incredibly hardworking and protective of the whole family. She seems to be taking over the vacancy of matriarch vacated by my Mum. There are never enough hours in the day for Lewis. So busy, and a talented Grime Artist in his own right – not my genre, but the skill of his lyrics is amazing. I remain eternally proud of them both.

All my other friends old and new. Our social life is busier now than it has ever been. **Mel,** a great friend when I needed her most, still missed over five years on.

My wonderful wife Wendy. For pushing me on to get this into print. The true love of my life. From the moment we met it was always you. Truly, Madly, Deeply.

Chris Brown (Browner). He knows a thing or two about writing. His comments and assistance is greatly appreciated.

Finally, **Bristol Rovers FC.** For the emotional rollercoaster that being a Gashead brings. For all the downs, the incredible highs have been worth it. Up the Gas, Rovers 'til I die.

The Tote End

In full song, *circa* mid '70s

Learning Curve: the trip to Orient, 1977

Promotion again. The Memorial Stadium: what a great early wedding gift

Promotion back to the League, Wembley, 2015, with Darrell Clarke

The pitch invasion after beating Dagenham and Redbridge to achieve consecutive promotions

Top, our Chairman, Wael al Qadi, carried shoulder-high outside the Queen Vic and (above) Darrell Clarke, the manager who brought us back from the abyss

www.ingramcontent.com/pod-product-compliance
Lightning Source LLC
Chambersburg PA
CBHW042046280426
43661CB00114B/1457/J